HarperCollins*West*

A Division of HarperCollinsPublishers

A Tehabi Book

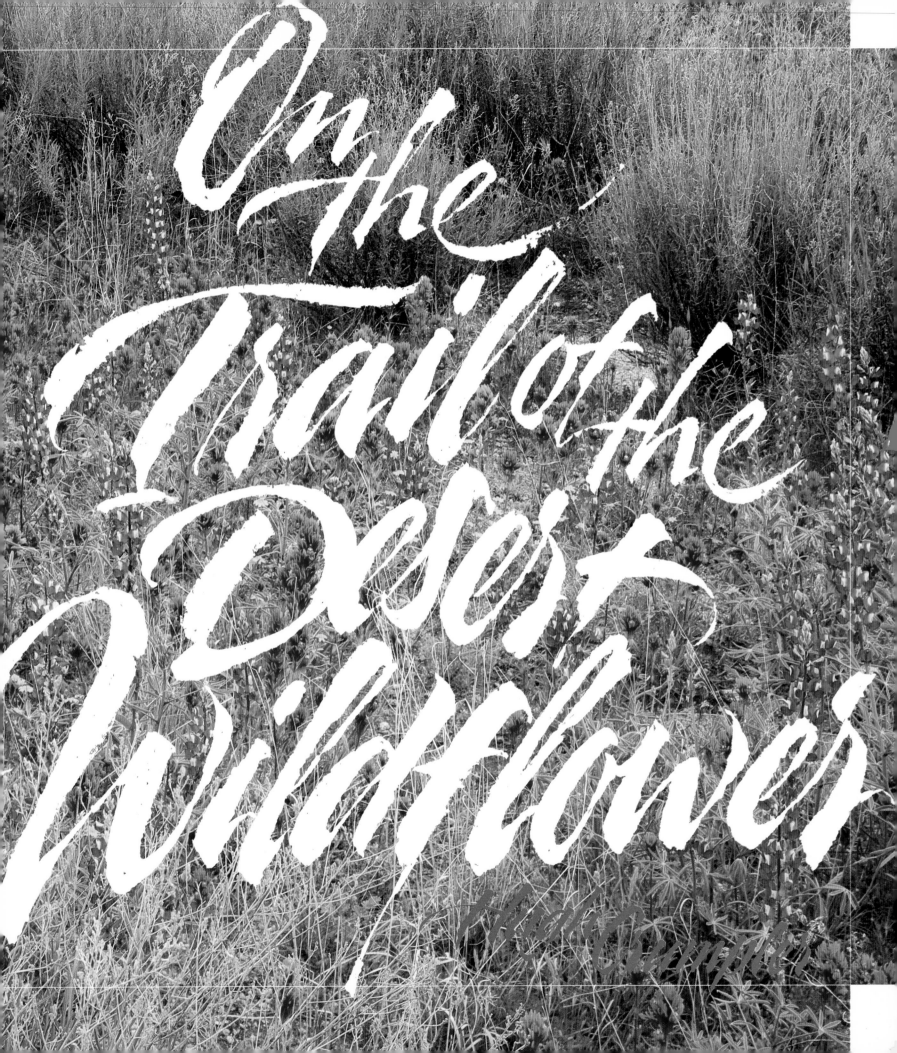

On the
Trail of the
Desert
Wildflower

Library of Congress Cataloging-in-Publication Data
Crumpler, Hugh.
On the Trail of the Desert Wildflower / Hugh Crumpler. — 1st ed.
p. cm.
Includes index.
ISBN 0-06-258528-2 (alk. paper) : $24.95
1. Desert plants—Southwest. New. 2. Wild flowers—Southwest. New. 3. Desert
plants—Southwest. New—Pictorial works. 4. Wild flowers—Southwest. New—Pictorial
works. 5. Desert plants—Southwest. New—Folklore. 6. Wild flowers—Southwest.
New—Folklore. 7. Folklore—Southwest. New. I. Title.
QK142.C7 1994
582.13'0979'09154—dc20

93-41266
CIP

For additional information contact:
HarperCollins Publishers, Inc.
10 East 53rd Street
New York, New York 10022

On the Trail of the Desert Wildflower
is one of the first books we have produced
for HarperCollins West. As such, we are
extremely grateful for the complete
confidence and full support we have
received from Clayton Carlson, Joann
Moschella, Jo Beaton and Beth Weber.
We are also deeply indebted to Hugh
Crumpler for allowing us to share his
wonderful experiences throughout the
deserts of America. We are equally
appreciative for the fabulous photography
provided by Willard and Kathy Clay,
Kathleen Norris Cook, Jeff Garton, Paul
Johnson and Tom Till. A special thanks,
as well, to Nancy Cash, our managing
editor, and Gilbert and Alison Voss,
technical editors, who held every detail of
the project together. — TEHABI BOOKS

On the Trail of the Desert Wildflower
was developed and produced by Tehabi
Books, San Diego, CA. Nancy Cash,
Editor; Sam Lewis, Art Director;
Tom Lewis, Editorial and Design
Director; Chris Capen, President.

FRONT COVER:
Prickly Pear, OPUNTIA PHAEACANTHA
INSIDE COVERS:
California Poppy, ESCHSCHOLZIA CALIFORNICA
FACING INSIDE FRONT COVER:
Cane Cholla, OPUNTIA IMBRICATA
TITLE PAGE:
Blue Lupines, LUPINUS,
Owl's Clover, ORTHOCARPUS *spp.*
THIS PAGE:
Saguaro, CEREUS GIGANTEUS

Contents

The typical vista that unfolds before the desert visitor is like an empty stage waiting for actors. Warm earth tones reach to the horizon. The golden sun rides overhead in a turquoise sky and paints a dramatic patina on the face of the land.

In the desert, the stage is always set and the curtain is always up – crying out for a splash of color, a bright surprise to jolt the audience. Perhaps, that is why the gods made wildflowers.

Anticipation of unexpected pleasures like the rising of a full moon or the emergence of night-blooming blossoms keeps me returning to the deserts. The clean, clear air enhances the illusion of the great size projected by the moon as it rises against the vast nighttime emptiness of the desert.

American deserts are so big and so broad that their pleasures are accessible to most would-be visitors. But what defines a desert? Definitions can be agonizingly technical. But all experts agree that deserts are dry, generally receiving ten inches or less of precipitation yearly, and are subject to ten inches or more evaporation. Those two factors together spell d-e-s-e-r-t.

Aridity is just about the only feature that is common to all deserts. Even the names given to deserts can vary as do the common names of flowers, depending on where you're from. The five major North American deserts are known to some as the Sonoran, Mojave, Great Basin, Chihuahuan, and Painted Desert (sometimes referred to as the Colorado

A solitary red spike of Indian Paintbrush, CASTILLEJA sp. pushed through the sharp, green lances of a Yucca, YUCCA sp. Nature's coupling of the rugged Yucca and the gentle Indian Paintbrush could have been the result of **PETALS AND THORNS** *an afternoon's careful composition by a Van Gogh. Elegant though it appears to be, Paintbrush can be something of a bully. It sometimes fastens onto the roots of another plant and becomes a parasite.*

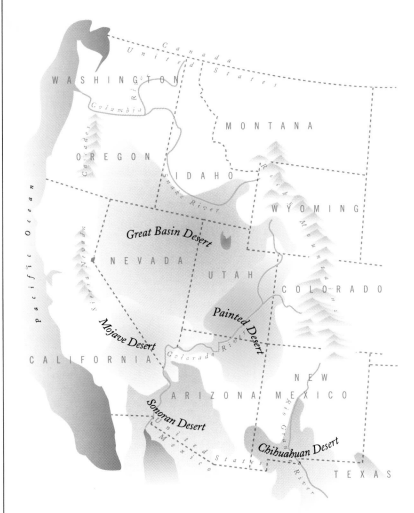

Desert). But whether we're talking about the Sonoran or any of these deserts, each is as unique as it is beautiful.

I have walked along the Colorado River banks, green ribbons laced with mesquite and willow, and marveled. Marveled that one of the world's great rivers, the liquid lifeline of the West, touches four of America's five **ARID BEAUTY** great deserts. Half a mile from the cold, blue water, lies a land of Creosote Brush and Chuckwallah, sand and Cactus, Catsclaw and Sidewinder – a land called Desert. I have walked in high deserts and low deserts, in hot deserts and cold deserts. I have seen deserts with forty-foot evergreen Pinyon Pines and deserts sparsely covered with low-growing Sage. I have walked in deserts that flow flat as a tabletop before falling off the distant horizon, and have seen deserts that come to a jarring halt at the base of ten thousand foot mountains. I have walked to quick exhaustion across barren sand dunes and have set buoyant steps along an arroyo carpeted in spring wildflowers. But the most useful definition of a desert is the definition that comes as the result of your own experiences in this wondrous land.

I once came upon a lone Desert Lily, HESPEROCALLIS UNDULATA, in the desert Badlands. The flower was so isolated from other living things that it had taken on the neutral color of the desert. Not the white or green of a lily. Betrayed by its seclusion, had it forgotten how to be a lily? Gray while composing his "Elegy" perhaps had such a lily in mind: Full many a flower is born to blush unseen, And waste its sweetness on the desert air.

Hugh Crumpler

flowers
Sonoran
Desert

The first time I walked in a forest of Saguaro — Giant Cactus, as it is commonly called — I was increasingly perplexed by one of those pestering mental ghosts that flicker around in the mind without taking a form that can be expressed. So I stopped in the pencil of shade laid down by a 25-foot Saguaro trunk. Something's missing from this landscape, I thought. Then the mental ghost took solid form. Solid and gigantic.

What's missing here, I announced to an audience of cactus, are dinosaurs. This is a primevalscape, I said, not an earthscape. These ribbed, green columns are not trees. They stand here naked. They grow in forests. Yet, no fallen leaves cushion my footsteps on the forest floor. This Giant Cactus, I announced, is unfulfilled. It needs rampaging herds of *Tyrannosaurus Rex*, *Ankylosaurus*, and other slashing species of thunder lizards. Then it could pass for a genuine primeval land.

The ancient Tohono O'odam Indians (also called Papago) held Saguaro Cactus in such high esteem that they dated their calendar from the beginning of the Saguaro harvest. And no wonder the Tohono O'odam looked in awe at the Saguaro. Merely its physical presence is overwhelming. It is a columnar storage tank for water, rising to a height of as much as fifty feet. It grows as a single column, or with branches like a tree. In the early stages of growth the new branches, emerging from the trunk, look like great hairy warts.

For the Tohono O'odam, the Saguaro was a primary source of food. The Indians used long poles to harvest the Saguaro "apples" that ripen in mid-summer. The fruit is sweet and nutritious and is eaten raw or stewed. Women ground the seeds in stone *morteros* to produce Saguaro butter. A single Saguaro Cactus could produce over 400,000 seeds in a season. Much to the dismay of Father Francisco

The Saguaro, CARNEGIEA GIGANTEA, is wonderfully engineered for the conservation of water. The plant is deeply ribbed and the ribs are covered

SAGUARO

with inch-and-a-half, keep-away needles. The ribs respond like bellows or like pleats in a drape. They allow the trunk to expand as the plant absorbs water through its wide network of shallow roots, or to contract as it uses the stored water. Its green, waxy skin inhibits evaporation in the hot, desert air. Below: Blossoms cap the arm of a Saguaro.

Following page:

The mighty Saguaro pierce the desert floor like giant thorny

SAGUARO FOREST *pencils.*

Standing as if they were monuments to a forgotten age, the Saguaro is protected by law and found only in the Sonoran.

Hermenegildo Garces, an eighteenth century missionary and enthusiastic desert wanderer, the Tohono O'odam also fermented a strong drink from Saguaro. He considered Saguaro wine to be as pernicious as the *mezcal* brewed from Agave or Century Plant.

Saguaro flowers blossom from the top of the plant's egg-shaped fruit. The blossoms are white, with a yellow center. They are waxy in appearance, shaped somewhat like roses. Night-blooming, the Saguaro depends largely on bats and beetles for pollenization.

Arizona named the Saguaro its state flower as it grows only in Arizona and in a few places along the Colorado River in the Sonoran Desert of California. It is the largest of our cactus and is a cactus of superlatives — a wonder of America, a plant to match its people.

Wonders abound in the desert, as I am constantly reminded. Aphrodite must have walked this way, I thought, as I came into view of **MEXICAN GOLD POPPY** Mexican Gold Poppies that had turned the desert slope into a carpet of shimmering gold. Aphrodite, goddess of love and desire, came to mind because, as the Greek myth reveals, flowers sprang up wherever she trod the earth.

The poppies grew in such profusion and in such universal perfection that divine magic seemed a possibility. On reflection I entertained an alternative: several inches of winter and spring rain had been most helpful.

In Mexico this poppy is known by the charming name of *Amapola del Campo* — Poppy of the Countryside — because of its habit of laying down sheets of gold following springtime rains. The flowers are four-petaled, cup-shaped, and orange-yellow in color. The foot-high plants bear blue-green, fernlike leaves.

Another flower that carpets sections of the desert from southern Arizona to western Texas and much of Mexico is the Desert Poppy. But this fellow is traveling on a fake passport. The plant, a creeper, is not a poppy at all. But the flower looks enough like a poppy to be mistaken for one.

Flowers of the Desert Poppy are cup-shaped and brilliant orange. The blossoms face sunward at the ends of stalks which grow above the creepers. Those creepers are forked and

"Amapola" is Spanish for "poppy." "Amapola" in song and word is the beautiful señorita in every village of the Mexican countryside. The rich orange-yellow petals, a little shorter than the long petaled California Poppy, open wide to drink in the sunshine. The Mexican Gold Poppy, ESCHSCHOLZIA MEXICANA, beautifies the desert slopes much as the shy señorita brings beauty to the village.

hairy. In addition to covering great areas of the desert when in bloom, the Desert Poppy frequently pops up as a roadside flower.

The California Poppy is the state flower of California and is truly a captive of the sun. When the sun goes down, or is covered by clouds, the California Poppy twists each of its blossoms into tight rolls. They then open again in full sunshine.

Poppies are not, however, the only ones who use the sun as a pointer. A bearded old-timer who said he had spent years prospecting the desert bragged about how he was never lost. He could always find his way because he knew the secret of the Barrel Cactus. It was as good as a compass because it always leaned toward the south. I too had noticed that mature Barrel Cactus always lean away from vertical, but I never paid any attention to what direction.

The beauty of fields of California Poppy, Eschscholzia **CALIFORNIA POPPY** Once I used a pocket compass myself, to check out the old-timer's *California, is legendary. Early* desert lore. Most of them did lean in the general direction of south, but not due south. Some *Spanish sailors, awed by the* southeast, some southwest. I even found some big ones on a canyon wall that leaned north. *sight of California Poppy fields* But the truth of the matter is, it's the source of light that attracts Barrel Cactus.

that spread from the shores to the Perhaps it can't be used as a compass, but it had other unique uses. *horizon, called the country "the* During the Great American Depression of the 1930's, people used the needles of Barrel *land of fire." Its cup-shaped* Cactus in their windup victrolas. In the hippie years of the 1960's something happened to *flower is responsible for one of the* the red-flowering Peyote Cactus of the Chihuahuan Desert. Peyote, also known in Texas as *Spanish names — copa de oro, or* Drywhisky, almost disappeared. Seekers of unreality dug up the little plants, and cut and *"cup of gold."* dried the "buttons" from the turnip-size taproots. The eating of Peyote "buttons" produces intense hallucinations, and has long been a part of the ceremonies of several Native American tribes.

Cactus, I have decided after many encounters, is a plant with conflicting personalities. Good guy, bad guy. Hero, villain. Always ambivalent. Take, for example, the three features most commonly noted about the cactus: flowers, fruit, and spines. The flowers are divine, the fruit is delicious, and the spines are devilish. What kind of a Dr. Jekyll/Mr. Hyde, do we have here?

For one thing, cactus defines the desert. The desert is the Commonwealth of the

Barrel Cactus plants squat on the desert slopes like green fireplugs left standing after the city has been blasted.

BARREL CACTUS

Barrel Cactus, FEROCACTUS spp., would certainly look lost anywhere except the desert, where it is at home with other strange plants. Much desert lore centers on the reported lifesaving quality of Barrel Cactus. It is

said to be a living canteen -- full of water waiting to be tapped by the thirsty traveler. But getting the liquid is not as easy as the stories indicate. Tapping a Barrel Cactus requires use of a heavy tool -- like an axe or a machete -- to chop off the top. Then the workman must hollow out a place for the liquid to accumulate. The drink? Not very satisfying and maybe less liquid than the chopper lost in sweat.

Cacti, for no other plant is as widespread in all the American deserts. It is somewhat misleading, however, that the towering Saguaro — the giant American cactus — has become the marque of the American deserts. Misleading because the Saguaro grows only in a limited part of the Sonoran Desert. On the other hand, Prickly Pear and an estimated 2,000 other species of cactus grow in all the American deserts. But none have the majesty of the Saguaro.

A widespread cactus with no majesty is the Cholla (rhymes with Soya). The Cholla is the guerrilla of the desert — the sneaky alley fighter who would as soon fell a friend as an enemy. The common name is Jumping Cholla. Desert lore says the name came from the Indians, who believed that Cholla joints — either those fallen to the ground or those still growing on the plant — actually leap onto a passing person or animal and hang on by their hooked spines.

Among the Chollas, Chain Cholla is noteworthy because its fruits **JUMPING CHOLLA** hang in chain-like clusters, increasing in size year after year. Sometimes the chain becomes so long that a string of fruit touches the ground. Another with a similar-sounding name is Cane Cholla. This cactus got its name from its long, slender branches — resembling canes or walking sticks. Its fruit is lemon yellow and its flower is usually purple. Cane Cholla fruit is probably the tastiest produced by the Chollas. Indians of the Chihuahuan Desert roasted the fruit in fire pits and stored it for later use.

Although several of the Chollas are called Jumping Cholla, the best-known of the Jumping Chollas is Teddy Bear Cholla. The name comes from the fact that the plant appears, from a distance, to be covered with fur — an illusion created by the spines. And the stubby branches resemble the arms and legs of a teddy bear. Don't be misled, though, Teddy Bear Cholla is not something to pick up and cuddle. I doubt that any amount of cactus sensitivity training could change my view of Jumping Cholla. It is ugly. The flower and the fruit are sickly green, sometimes sickly white. The plant, afflicted with drooping black and brown branches, looks half-dead. Teddy Bear Cholla is as friendly as a rattlesnake. Ambush is its favorite tactic. It is the bushwhacker of the cacti family. Teddy Bear Cholla is the cactus from Hell.

Teddy Bear Cholla, OPUNTIA BIGELOVII, grows from a single, tree-like trunk. Short, stubby branches grow in clusters at the top of the trunk and are covered with an **JUMPING CHOLLA** *infinity of barbed spines. The jointed branches are only slightly attached. The lightest contact enables the joint to secure a grip and break away from the mother plant. The victim has then become the habitation of a golf-ball sized problem. No tool has been invented that plucks Cholla needles without surgery.*

Following page: Silver Cholla, OPUNTIA ECHINOCARPA, and Barrel Cactus, **SILVER CHOLLA** *FEROCACTUS ACANTHODES, cohabit along rocky ridges and down into palm-studded ravines. Palms make an oasis of shade in blistering desert valleys.*

Jumping from the treacherous to the sublime, I spotted a butterfly bush — an animated painting of orange, brown and white aerial dancers — and stopped beside the trail. A troupe of Painted Ladies, famous for mass migrations, had selected a fragrant Desert Lavender bush as a feeding stop on their perilous journey north from Baja California. The chorus of butterflies performed a fluttery ballet around the Desert Lavender. A philharmonic of wild honeybees provided a soft accompaniment. The music of the honeybees, sharing the desert nectar with the Painted Ladies, was a softly insistent hum. It was a one-note symphony played on a hundred strings. The Painted Ladies had chosen wisely, for the sweetest of nectars collects in the clover-like blossoms of Desert Lavender. Desert Lavender is one of the common shrubs of the desert. In some years, though, its beauty is easily overlooked. At that time, the flowers are so pale that they blend in with the gray-greens of the woolly-leaved shrub.

In the season of my walk, the lovely shrub had manufactured a lavish display of deep lavender blossoms. The clouds of its **DESERT LAVENDER** perfume were a homing signal to the butterflies. Here in the clear desert air, that faint scent explained why Lavender, perhaps the most feminine of aromas, is a favored fragrance in European boudoirs.

In a way, the butterfly bush was a bonus. But by that standard, the desert is filled with bonuses. Every trip turns up a few of them. I had hit the trail that morning to visit a small stand of Elephant Trees, one of the rare plants of the Sonoran Desert. As I walked by the butterfly bush, the startled Painted Ladies filled the air with fluttering spots of diaphanous colors. They danced past me to embrace a field of blindingly white Chicory flowers in bloom on the hillside.

The half dozen elephant trees I was interested in grew in a small area of a boulder strewn dry wash. Looking at these strange, 12-foot trees, it was easy enough to see why they had baffled botanists and plant hunters. Elephant Trees were not identified in the American Sonoran Desert until 1937. The tiny, white flowers — no wider than the fingernail of a lady's pinky — could not be called showy. But it is not the flowers that have drawn attention

Frost and snow in the desert? They appear to be contradictions in terms because we think of the desert as hot. But snow and frost come to all the **ICE COVERED VEGETATION** *deserts, although not to all parts of the deserts and not in all cold seasons. Desert cold has a special invigorating quality because it occurs with low humidity. Try a walk in the desert at 40 degrees. It is a bracing wakeup call.*

The Desert Lavender, HYPTIS EMORYI, is a subtle looking shrub, its whitish foliage almost blending into the surrounding landscape. But its sweet aromatic lavender scent quickly brings it into focus. Its tiny lavender flowers clustered on tall erect stems tempt many a bee and butterfly.

to this strange tree. That feature is the "elephant trunk" appearance of the tree trunk and its branches. From a thick base the trunk and limbs taper only slightly, then abruptly end like an elephant trunk.

I pulled off a piece of white peeling bark to a thin layer of green, followed by a layer of red bark. Using a warm boulder as a backrest, I examined the strips of bark. A small, Side-blotched Lizard scurried across the sand. In the theater of my imagination I watched a pageant among the Elephant Trees and remembered the story of Chinigchinich, a Cahuilla *shaman* born long before the arrival of the Spaniards, who kneeled at the trunk of an Elephant Tree. Chinigchinich was so wise that he founded a sect whose followers spread far beyond his own tribe to native peoples of many clans in the mountains and the desert. The near-naked *shaman* drew a flint knife, and made grooves through the layers of bark in a ceremony of exact patterns. Blood-red sap of the Elephant Tree filled the grooves. The **ELEPHANT TREE** stern, gray-haired leader rolled the gummy sap into balls and placed them in a rabbitskin pouch. He turned back toward the mountains, now possessing the strongest of medicines.

Further along the trail I came upon great forests of Mescal which stood tall and erect on the boulder-strewn slopes of Ghost Mountain. Mescal, or Agave, or Desert Century Plant, resembles an elongated stalk of green asparagus as it reaches maturity in late spring. Then it sprouts more than a dozen flower clusters that grow close to the stalk and face upward like a stairway of sun-worshipers. Some observers find resemblance to a candelabra at this stage of the plant's life.

Mescal begins its unusual life as a rosette of thick, rigid, lance-shaped leaves. When the plant is about a dozen years old, the stalk bursts from the rosette and begins rapid growth — as much as five inches in 24 hours — to a height of 10-14 feet. The stalk produces its clusters of yellow flowers and the flowers create seeds. On the dry desert slopes where Mescal prospers, its life is 12 to 20 years. The old, familiar legend tells us that the cycle of life and death occurs once every hundred years — hence, the name Century Plant. The legend derives from a seed of truth: the plant blooms only once and dies after flowering.

The Mescal plantations of Ghost Mountain are populated with both the stately,

Antonio Garra, paramount capitan of a little band of Kupa at the village of the Hot Springs, used the holy sap of the Elephant Tree, BURSERA MICROPHYLLA, to recruit Native Americans for his war against the new American rulers of California. But even a talisman as strong as the blood gum of the Elephant Tree did not bring victory. After a year of rebellion, Antonio Garra's war ended with his death before an American firing squad in 1852.

The formidable Mescal (*AGAVE PALMERI* and also the *A. PARRYI*) is a noble provider. Called by many names, Desert Century Plant, Agave, this desert plant was a source of food as well as fiber rope and crude clothing material used by many Native American peoples. "A-moosh" was a Mescal food made of the first two feet of the green stalk. Baked overnight in a firepit covered with dirt or sand, it had a flaver as sweet as sorghum molasses, or baked pineapple.

MESCAL

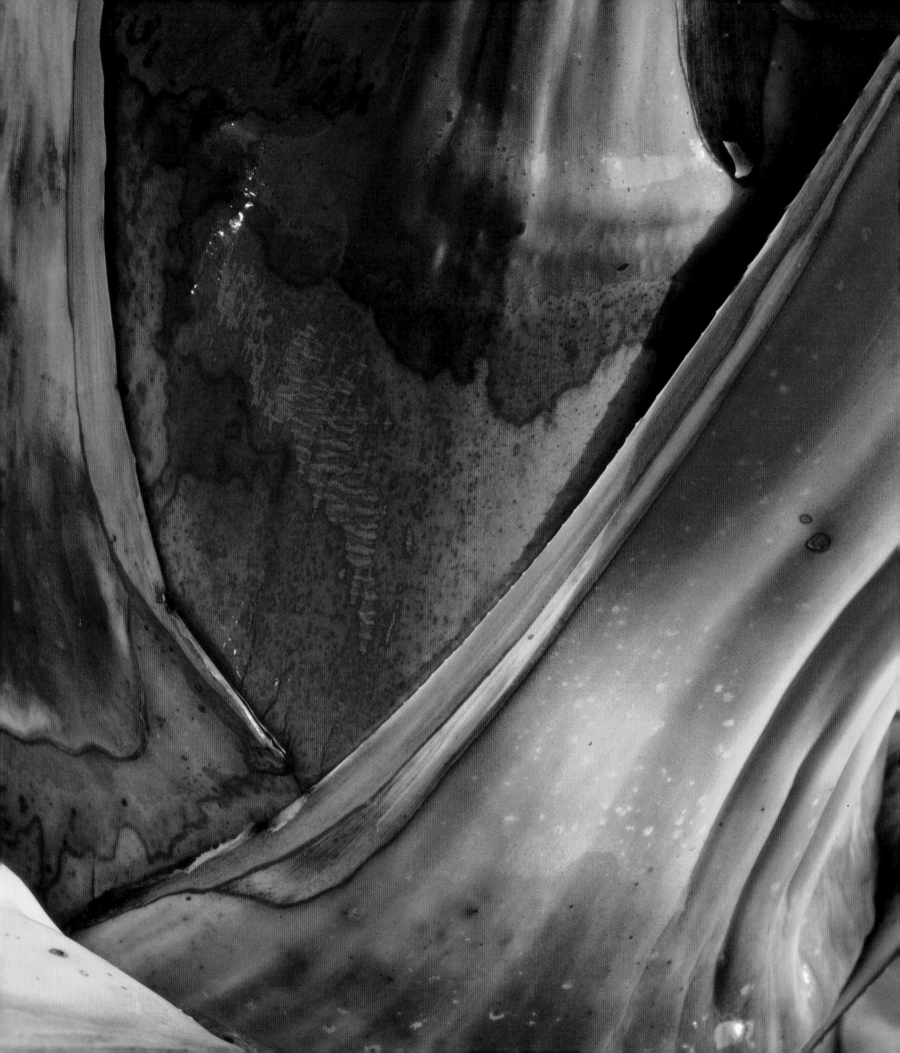

living Mescal plants and the dead, sun-bleached bones of last season's Century plants. Viewing that sharp contrast between the living and the dead is one of the pleasures that calls me to a walk up Ghost Mountain every spring.

The difference between life and death is often but an illusion in a desert that is filled with some of the strangest shaped plants on earth. An early desert traveler described the strange Ocotillo plant as being "like a bunch of buggy whips stuck in the sand." The oddities of the Ocotillo are numerous. It is the only member of its plant family, although there are some 11 species of the genus found in the deserts and drylands of the United States and Mexico.

I walked one day through a desert slope covered with Ocotillo. The funnel-shaped plants composed of numerous straight and slender wands were brown, the lifeless brown of dead plants. Even as I watched, rain clouds formed on the horizon. The clouds moved across the desert and emptied a drenching rainfall on the dry sands. The Ocotillo was transformed. The next day, the **OCOTILLO** graceful wands were covered with tiny green leaves. Later, when the soil dried, the tiny leaves died and fell. Each falling leaf left a trace of leaf stalk that developed into a slightly-curved thorn.

In one continuous cycle of life-and-death, the Ocotillo had armored **MESCAL** itself with the prickly briars that are essential to the survival of so many desert plants. The Ocotillo's chameleon-like change — triggered by soil moisture — can occur several times during a season. Ocotillo reaches the perfection of its feral beauty when the tips of the wands burst into tight clusters of blood-red flowers touched with yellow. The tubular, one-inch flowers are crowded together, peering skyward, in queues of ten or more. As the plant grows taller — as high as thirty feet, but averaging about ten — the flexible wands turn downward, forming the distinctive funnel shape.

I have admired many Ocotillo fences, standing like soldiers in single file, in the yards and gardens of Mexican farmers in the Sonoran Desert along the Sea of Cortez. Farmers chop Ocotillo wands into equal lengths and plant them, almost touching. When the soil contains enough

The fibers of the long, tough Mescal, AGAVE DESERTI, rosette leaves provided the Indians with material for breechcloths, girdles, and sandals. As late as the early part of the Twentieth Century, a desert traveler described Mescal saddleblankets he had seen in use around Palm Springs. The maguey plant used in Mexico to make tequila is similar to the Mescal of the desert. Both are members of the Agave family.

Following page:

Ocotillo, FOUGUIERIA SPLENDENS, was a favorite campfire fuel of native peoples, cowboys, soldiers, prospectors, and Sonoran horse traders. Because of its high wax content, Ocotillo burns with a hot, white flame. This quality of Ocotillo gave it the old name of Candlewood. Another popular name, though seldom heard today, is Coach-Whip. Indians of the Southwest, who overlooked no source of food, ate both the flowers and the seed.

moisture, the transplanted wands go through the leafing and shedding metamorphosis that they undergo when growing from the crown of a whole Ocotillo plant. A green fence without paint. With no tool but a machete and no technology other than the hard-won knowledge of nature, the Mexican farmer creates a living fence — a barbed barrier, a slender monument to the ingenuity of necessity.

When the swirling, changing currents of a windstorm blow across the desert, I have seen Ocotillo turn into a wild and savage thing, more beast than vegetable. The elastic wands, anchored in the crown at ground level writhe and twist like the serpents that served as Medusa's hair. The red flowers at the tips of the branches could be the **ORGAN PIPE** darting tongues of probing serpents.

The Organ Pipe Cactus, though not as intimidating as the Ocotillo, is more of a treat for the tongue. Its fruit is so delicious that generations of Tohono O'odham and Pima Indians of the Sonoran Desert of Arizona and Mexico have camped out among the plants at harvest time and feasted on *Pitahaya Dulce* until the season ended. In addition to eating the ripe fruit as it is dislodged from the cactus with forked poles, the Indians sun-dry it for storage and use it throughout the year. The Papago make both a wine and a beer from the fruit of Organ Pipe.

The name Organ Pipe Cactus is a felicitous description of the plant's appearance. Strong, slender columns branch from the base and grow straight up and bunched together. The plant can reach a height of twenty feet. Pale, trumpet-shaped flowers bloom from the sides of the columns. The flowers rich in nectar open at night, attracting bats, birds, and beetles. During the daylight hours, bees and hummingbirds join in the harvest until the flowers close. When an Organ Pipe Cactus dies, its skeleton is harvested by the Tohono O'odham for building material and fuel. After the skin and watery pulp disappear, the supporting skeleton of the columns is white and bone-like. Perforations make it light in weight, but the bones are strong and enduring.

In the United States, Organ Pipe, STENOCEREUS THURBERI, grows in a relatively small area. That area is made up of 510 square miles of the Organ Pipe Cactus National Monument and 4,560 square miles of the adjoining Papago Reservation. Both the Monument and the Reservation are in Southern Arizona with borders on Mexico. The plant appears in much larger numbers in Mexico's Sonoran Desert.

*flowers
Mojave
Desert*

A great white beast, an alien to the blistering Mojave Desert, lumbered along in slow-motion through a forest of strange, leafless trees whose limbs seemed to be gesticulating wildly in every direction. Two dozen more of the singular animals followed in Indian file behind the leader. As they walked, the exotic quadrupeds sank hock-deep in a golden carpet of small, many-petalled flowers.

The animals of the exotic caravan were two-humped, Bactrian camels of Asia. In the year 1857 they had plodded across the continent from Texas to California following a gigantic white Bactrian known as Old Saeed. Leader of the camel expedition was Edward Fitzgerald Beale (1822-1893) — naval officer, war hero, explorer, rancher, Indian commissioner, trail blazer, and road builder — who had been commissioned by the United States to determine if camels were a practical answer to the problems of military transportation in the hot, sprawling deserts of the American Southwest.

When Beale proudly rode into Fort Tejon, California at the head of his spitting, belching animals — each carrying a 700-pound load — he was certain the camels had proved themselves. (And they were used as pack animals with some success.) But Beale's camels fell victim to the prejudices of mule-skinners and oxen teamsters. Also prejudiced against camels were horses, mules, burros, pigs, chickens, and cattle. They all tended to stampede upon the appearance of those long-legged beasts of the Gobi Desert. Soon enough, the government gave up on the noble experiment and sold off the camels to the more adventurous and daring among ranchers, miners, and cowboys. Within a few years, all the camels had disappeared.

And though Beale's camels are gone, I occasionally come across "camel tracks" in the desert. I had concluded that the tracks were made by the action of "dust

The Joshua Tree, YUCCA BREVIFOLIA, is as resilient as a "bronco-thrown" cowboy, it bounces right back after frost and cold --disasters that would doom many other desert plants. Snow sometimes falls in the high desert at the same time the Joshua Tree is in bloom. The Joshua Tree then becomes a patinated candelabra dusted with swansdown.

JOSHUA TREE

devils," tiny whirlwinds that rearrange the surface sands. But I never claimed I have unlocked all the mysteries of the desert.

The forest of strange, leafless trees that Beale's camels marched through on the way to Fort Tejon were not trees at all. They were Yucca plants, members of the Agave family, popularly known as the Joshua Tree. Their distinctive appearance has made them the trademark of the Mojave Desert. Joshua Trees were so baptized by early settlers who looked at these strange, cactus-like, plants and compared them to Joshua pointing the way out of the desert to the Promised Land. Others saw the dramatic gesticulations of a prophet in the many configurations of the Joshua Tree's branches.

It is no wonder that the desert pioneers thought that Yucca was a tree. Joshua Trees grow to a height of 50 feet and they most commonly grow, like many real trees, in forests of their own kind. When the Joshua Tree is in bloom, it is of surprising beauty. Surprising because the plant is ungainly and awkward — at least it would be if it tried to move. But in the springtime, the Joshua Tree blossoms with foot-long clusters of creamy-white flowers at the tips of its branches. Some have compared the texture and color of Joshua Tree blooms to ancient ivory.

A Joshua Tree in bloom supplies one of the delights of the desert. Year-round, every Joshua Tree is a self-contained community. It supports a menagerie of wildlife: woodpeckers, flickers, beetles, titmice, owls, ants, termites — even a tiny reptile, the desert night lizard, that is born in the tree and never leaves it.

The desert is inscribed with many life and death symbols. The sun, my constant companion, is the paramount symbol of life. In sharp contrast are the symbols of death — snow, frost and bleaching bones. They are white. And the color white itself is the preferred dress of death.

I have been stopped in my tracks by two of the desert's more spectacular flowering plants, a Jimson Weed and Prickly Poppy. Both fly white pennants that might well say: "Beware, you creatures of warm

---

Yuccas, YUCCA spp., are one of the desert's most versatile plants. Unlike its cousin, the Agave, the Yucca does not die after blooming, but continues to **YUCCA** *bloom year after year. Many of the species are edible, its buds, blossoms and fruit can be eaten raw or cooked, while others provide medicines and soap.*

To the earth-loving Mojave,
Cahuilla, Chemehuevi and other
desert Indians, the coming of the
Moon of Cactus Flowers
signified more than the aesthetic
pleasure brought to the Joshua
Tree forest by the bountiful
blossoms. The Indians plucked
the buds and blossoms, roasted
them in fire pits and feasted on
the sweet harvest.

In addition to supplying food, the

YUCCA

Yucca, YUCCA SCHIDIGERA (member of the Agave family), supplied the native peoples with fiber for weaving, wood for fires, and building materials. The tough leaves were split and used for weaving baskets, for rough clothing and mats, and as thatch for roofs. The thorny spine at the end of the leaf made a handy sewing needle, complete with self-attached fiber thread.

blood, for here lies agony and death!" The two plants, carrying the deaths-head symbolism to still another level, flourish not only in deserts, but also in other wastelands, such as abandoned barnyards, ditches, and empty lots. But nature is contrary. The flowers of these deadly plants offer life-giving nectar to hungry ants, beetles, bees, and other insects. And that's not all. Jimson Weed, the Toloache of Indian lore, had a role in the rites of passage practiced by Indians of the American Southwest.

Toloache, a word descended straight from the Aztecs' language, was the name for the Indian brew doled out in careful dosages at the ceremony for boys entering into manhood. To a lesser degree it was also used in the rites for a girl completing passage to womanhood. Jimson Weed, a member of the deadly nightshade family, is poisonous in all its parts. Pharmaceutical wisdom handed down through many generations of medicine men did however, enable Indians to use Toloache in safe portions.

The narcotic effects of Toloache, DATURA WRIGHTII, were used by Native Americans to induce dreams that the Indians regarded as messages **TOLOACHE** *of universal wisdom, visions of life that remained with adolescent initiates in their passage from one life, childhood, to a second life, that of family-maker.*

The beauty of Jimson Weed lies in its snow-white, trumpet-shaped flower. The ten-inch trumpet often appears to have struggled through the rank growth of stalks and stems to burst into the sunlight. But its display is short-lived. With the appearance of the sun, the flower rapidly wilts. The seed-bearing fruit, the "apple" of Jimson Weed, is a round, prickly pod.

Your friends are probably talking about Jimson Weed when they refer to "Datura," "Sacred Datura," "Thorn Apple," "Indian Apple," "Mad Apple," Devil's Apple," or "Stinkweed." To add to the burden of its derisive names, Jimson Weed exudes a foul odor. In the language of the corral, it stinks. But few plants attract as many feeding insects as the three-inch, white flower of another deadly plant, the Prickly Poppy. Its quarter-size, yellow center is rich with nectar, so rich that I have seen it completely covered with wasps and beetles. Other insects waited on the silky, white petals for their turn at the honeypot.

The plant makes a formidable display

of thorns and stickers on all its parts except the flower. Only the most desperate animal will dare graze Prickly Poppies. Those that do are made ill by its toxic substances. If a milk animal — a cow or goat — eats it and survives, the toxins can be passed along to humans in the milk. As with so many other deadly plants, Native Americans found ways to use the Prickly Poppy as medicine. Comanche Indians steeped the seeds, found in the plant's thorny capsules, and used the liquid to treat sore eyes. Other Indians chewed the seeds to release painkilling narcosis. Their medical qualities, however, are more dangerous than healing. Practitioners of folk medicine have abandoned the use of Jimson Weed and Prickly Poppy because of their unpredictable and often deadly after-effects. To ranchers, Jimson Weed and Prickly Poppy are a couple of bad actors, to be rooted out wherever they appear.

While some actors sharing the desert stage are demure, others are flashy and more flamboyant. Even the noble grasses and flower-spent scrubbrush become dramatic expressions of form and color against the rugged desert landscape.

BROWSE SHRUBS

Radiant sunshine through luminescent desert air turns the leaves of shrubs into tablets of beaten gold -- like the golden tissue that Buddhist pilgrims buy to adorn their temples. Every image is possible on the slopes and washes of the desert. As the sun moves across the sky, it shadow-sculpts new forms and figures on the timeless landscape.

The first desert wildflower I could identify by sight was Brittlebush, golden crown of desert slopes and rocky places. It is a rounded bush with distinctive silvery-gray foliage all year round. When in flower, Brittlebush is even more distinctive. The golden flowers stand on long stems well above the bush. At that stage, Brittlebush is like a giant silvery pincushion filled with flower-tipped hatpins. Its two most distinctive features — silvery foliage and elevated flowers — make Brittlebush a plant easily identified in all seasons.

Incensio, the Spanish name for Brittlebush, should be a tip-off that something unusual is going on with this humble bush. That story takes us back to the Spanish period of California, the years when Spanish priests — first the Jesuits, then the Franciscans — built a chain of missions from the tip of Baja California to the bay of San Francisco. The Holy Fathers, the "Black Gowns" of the Native Americans, invited the heathen to worship, and the heathen came. The native peoples were impressed by the pomp and ceremony of the Catholic mass. The Catholic fathers, far from their home base in Spain, were dependant on shipments from Spain and the Philippines for essential church supplies that enabled them to carry on church ceremonials as they were performed everywhere in the civilized world.

Southwest Native American tribes: Apache, Navajo, Pima, and Tohono O'odam basket weavers, almost always women,

NATIVE AMERICAN BASKETRY

crafted containers weaving yucca, sumac, even mescal or agave fibers into baskets of all sizes and shapes. The exteriors were decorated with crushed juniper leaves or red ocher. The baskets were sometimes made water tight with melted pinyon pitch or plugged with leaves or wads of yucca root.

Once, so the legend goes, the yearly arrival of the Manila Galleon, supply ship of His Most Catholic Majesty's Indies fleet, was delayed by storms or pirates. The mission censers were empty. No incense was available for the swinging vessels that dispensed the sweet-smelling clouds of fragrance loved by the Indians. But all was not lost. A *Neophyte* — an Indian converted to Catholicism — appeared with a handful of yellow, gum nuggets. He told his Padre to burn them in the censers. The priests found the Brittlebush nuggets to be acceptable substitutes for the King's own Indies incense.

Mexican Indians, quick to find uses for the most ordinary objects, made a varnish from the gum of Brittlebush. They used both the gum and the resinous stems as fire-starters. Early desert travelers said Papago children used Brittlebush nuggets as chewing gum. And in New Mexico, Hispanic settlers called it **DESERT DANDELION** *MALACOTHRIX* **BRITTLEBUSH** *hierba del vaso* because they warmed the gum and spread it below the ribs (a part of the body called *vaso*) for relief of pain.

When I view a plant with the beauty and utility of Brittlebush, I can more nearly understand why Native Americans regarded many plants with a respect sometimes bordering on reverence. And while some plants are held in high esteem because of their spectacular beauty or usefullness, others are considered merely weeds. A case in point is the Dandelion. That is not a weed!

Edward Beale's two-humped, Asian camels were far from their natural element when they plodded through a carpet of the yellow Desert Dandelion in a Joshua Tree forest. The deserts of Asia and Africa — of the Old World in general — are surprisingly sparse in vegetation. The American deserts, by contrast, support a wide variety of vegetation year-round. When winter rains are timely, American deserts blossom into overflowing showcases of wildflowers.

Edward Beale's camel caravan could have browsed its way from El Paso to Los Angeles on the nutritious plants and shrubs of the desert. The frontier cavalry depended on native browse to supplement the grain they carried for horses and mules. Immigrant trains stopped for the night, whenever possible, where shrubs, trees, and plants provided feed for livestock. Many of the plants are those we know best as flowers.

When at its flowering peak, Brittlebush, ENCELIA FARINOSA, is a striking hemisphere of daisy-like, three-inch flowers. The color is golden yellow. In its preferred environment I have seen flowering Brittlebush glowing against the gray, rocky slopes like satellites flung to earth by the sun.

Following page: This Desert Dandelion, MALACOTHRIX GLABRATA, is not the pestilential weed, Common Dandelion, TARAXACUM OFFICINALE, that discourages lawn gardeners. It is a larger, separate genus. Like its eastern cousin, though, Desert Dandelions produce the familiar seed vehicles that John Burroughs called "a hundred fairy balloons."

Among the common ones of the desert is the Desert Dandelion. The dandelion has a characteristic it shares with a few other desert flowers — it bursts into bloom as a solid blanket of yellow that covers wide areas. I remember a Desert Dandelion jubilee that started in an abandoned vineyard of the Borrego Valley in California and seemed to spread its golden sheet to the distant Santa Rosa Mountains.

Many of my trips were like journeys into other worlds. I walked along Coyote Creek on an Autumn day that could have been designed by the gods for their own pleasure. A soft breeze blowing steadily down the canyon caressed my skin like the touch of satin. In its passage through the San Jacinto Mountains, the breeze had acquired an edge of high-altitude chill — just enough to add a nip, without discomfort, to a 70-degree day. It was the kind of bracing weather that causes men to drop the tools of field or factory and walk joyfully into the embrace of nature.

Walking up to the fragile beauty of a Desert Willow, CHILOPSIS LINEARIS, *flower is as unexpected as finding a Renoir in a thrift shop. No show off, the Desert Willow spaces its blossoms sparingly on its* **DESERT WILLOW** *open, airy foliage. Each large, orchid-like flower is a pastel gem in white, lavender and yellow.*

The sky was bigger and bluer than real, just **DESERT WILLOW BLOSSOM** *The distinctive, long, thin pod of the Desert Willow sways on the tree in cadence with the beating of the wind.* as it always appears on a clear day in desert country. Little Coyote Creek ran crystal and cold. The waters sang a muted, liquid song as they flowed across sand and gravel bottoms and along green banks. The graceful, weeping appearance of a Desert Willow tree caught my attention. I stepped across the creek, glancing at the sandy beach for bighorn sheep tracks. None.

The Desert Willow had caught my attention because it bore several lavender blossoms, long out of season. Desert Willow, which is not a true willow but a member of the Catalpa family, bears long graceful leaves. The flower is so much like an orchid in appearance but the slim, slightly-curved seed pods of the Desert Willow are its signature feature. I opened a mature seed pod that had ripened to the color of the sandy desert floor and was beginning to split along the seam. I counted 43 winged seeds in the nine-inch pod. The tree carried at least a hundred similar pods. That translated to more than 4,000 chances that the tree would reproduce itself in a single season.

In the harsh, desert climate, plants need every stratagem they can generate to insure survival and reproduction. The Desert Willow's strategy is a good one. Its pods ripen one-at-a-time over a long period, each pod launching several dozen winged seeds that travel haphazardly with the wind and the water into the fickle clasp of the desert.

My attention was diverted from the Desert Willow by a flash of color from a hovering hummingbird. I followed the bird and its flight led us to a Chuparosa bush. For the hummingbird, the Chuparosa was survival. For me, it was pleasure.

A pleasurable experience it was to find a Chuparosa laden with flowers. Daredevil hummingbirds flew cover over the bush like fighter planes over a bomber. If I were not fearful of stretching the metaphor too far I might have written that the hummingbirds were providing protection for the wild honeybees that feasted on the red flowers of the Chuparosa. But the hummingbirds were there at the Chuparosa bush for the same reason as the bees — to feast on the abundance of sweet nectar that wells up in the long cleft blossoms.

The Chuparosa, JUSTICIA CALIFORNICA, drops its small leaves after flowering. It then

CHUPAROSA

looks like a lifeless, twiggy shrub. But its red flowers are a cornucopia of nectar-rich blossoms. The loss of its leaves and exposure of the flowers is like opening the door to a hummingbird supermarket.

It is easy enough to immediately see that a honeybee crawls in and out of the flowers on a feeding spree. Hummingbirds, though, appear to be attacking the flowers. It is the nature of hummingbirds to re-create the antics of the Red Baron's Flying Circus. Over the Chuparosa, the hummingbirds hovered, dived, fed staccato-style on a host of blossoms. They flew backward and poised overhead in one place like a helicopter. Chuparosa flowers seem to bring out the most daring tactics of hummingbirds. While I watched, a purple-throated Costa's hummingbird drove away a larger, red-crowned Anna's hummingbird. The Chuparosa produced enough nectar for all. But the sharing protocol is alien to the hummingbird disposition.

The name Chuparosa comes from the Spanish of Mexico and means hummingbird (the Spanish *chupa rosa* meaning "rose sucker"). The hummingbird is a star player in the mythology and history of Hispanic America. Aztec warriors who died in battle or were sacrificed after capture first went to the House of the Sun. There they served in the honor guard of Huitzilopochtli, the morning sun, for four years. After that service they were reincarnated as earthly hummingbirds and spent eternity dining on heavenly nectar. In the Mexico of today, it is said, practitioners of the occult arts prescribe mummified hummingbirds as a magic altar at which evil spirits are pacified.

In the desert of today, the hummingbird — prickly-tempered survivor — is a stellar warrior, Guardian Angel of the red-flowering Chuparosa.

Off in the distance stands the skyline of Salt Lake City, earthly center of the Church of Jesus Christ of Latter-day Saints. The city was wrenched stone by stone from the wilderness by the Mormons who came to this desolate, arid country nearly two centuries ago. But only a few miles from the malls and pavement, we are in a desert, a land where rainfall measures less than ten inches yearly. It is the Great Basin Desert, America's largest and coldest desert.

This Great Basin is a land of Sagebrush, Saltbush, Greasewood, Horsebrush, and half-a-hundred other flowering shrubs that range in height from squat-down, to head-high and taller. Sagebrush predominates — Big Sagebrush, **SALTBUSH** Sand Sagebrush and Black Sagebrush. The Great Basin is cattle country to a large extent because the land is a cornucopia of nutritious grasses and plants. A litany of Great Basin grasses and browse plants could be set to music and played as a symphony of the desert: Cheatgrass and Blue Bunch **TUMBLEWEED** Wheatgrass, Buckwheat and Bottlebrush Squirreltail Grass, Rabbit Brush, Winter Wheatgrass and Indian Rice Grass, Shadscale, and Spiny Hopsage. Locoweeds grow here, too, their toxins poised to turn a grazing steer into a punchdrunk wanderer.

To the casual walker, the landscape of this high desert makes an initial impression of a static and monotonous carpet of gray-tan nothingness. Then a shoulder-high ball that appears to be constructed from a tangle of rusting barbed wire, rattles softly as it bounces across the trail, driven by a sharp wind from the Wasatch Mountains. It is Tumbleweed.

"Tumbleweed." What a marvelously descriptive home-made improvement on the colorless name, "Russian Thistle." Rolling, rolling, rolling, and dropping its seeds at

"Alkali" describes a soil that Westerners pronounce with the same disgust that they use when pronouncing "rattlesnake." It is soil that contains an excess of soluble salts. Alkali soils are usually white like snow. A few plants, like Saltbush, ATRIPLEX spp., and Winter Fat, CERATOIDES LANATA, prosper on alkali soils and are exceptionally nutritious browse for livestock and wild animals.

Following page: Tumbleweed, SALSOLA KALI var TENUIFOLIA, was accidentally introduced into the Southwest in the last century. Its rapid spread left ranchers sputtering in search of words to describe their aversion to this noxious pest. The rancher's wife on the treeless Great Plains, without a Christmas evergreen, whitewashed a tumbleweed, decorated it with gimcracks, and displayed it on a table. The wife of a neighboring rancher rode by to see the marvel of ingenuity. The whitewashed tumbleweed was gone. "If I hadn't trashed it," the lady explained, "That Old Cowboy of mine would have called off Christmas."

every turn — insolently shedding seeds within sight of the rancher who silently curses the thistle weeds that he knows will follow in the wake of the pestilential Tumbleweed. In song, in pictures, and in legend, the Tumbleweed is symbolic of the Great Basin, of the intermountain West. Which came first — the Tumbleweed careening across the plains or the lonely cowboy riding into an empty distance?

The desert holds many more surprises than the Tumbleweed, which is an alien plant that was accidentally introduced from a land of Cossacks and Commissars. To find the surprises, the unexpected, take your time and look closely. The desert is in no hurry. Its hostile appearance is a friendly warning: do not enter here unprepared.

Some of the desert's surprises are life-giving ones. None lived to tell that story with more conviction than those of Brigham Young's pioneers who survived the winter of 1847-'48, the cruel first winter. The Mormons worked on short rations and they prayed for deliverance from their Time of Starvation.

Rabbit Brush, CHRYSOTHAMNUS *NAUSEOSUS, is a plant of opportunity. Wherever the land is disturbed by fire or flood Rabbit Brush may be the*

RABBIT BRUSH

first new plant to appear. Rabbit Brush is a late-blooming beauty. In late summer, yellow flowers burst from its light, hairy stems. The rich yellow of Rabbit Brush flowers attracted the Navajo. They made a yellow dye and used it to decorate pottery and blankets.

It was the humble and peaceable Paiute Indians, the "Diggers" of Western history, who pointed to the desert and said, "Out there is food." The Indians led the Mormons to patches of wilted, brown, straplike leaves and with pointed sticks, hardened in sagebrush fires, the Indians unearthed familiar-looking bulbs a foot below the surface. The Mormons pitched in with their iron digging tools. The supply of bulbs seemed endless. The hungry settlers filled sacks and wagons. Boiled or baked, the bulbs tasted like onion with a touch of garlic. The lifegiving crop was the bulb of the Sego Lily, a flower that rises knee-high from a single stem, with slender leaves growing from the base of the stem. The white, bowl-shaped flower is painted with spots of yellow and purple at the center. The grateful Mormons of Utah had an even more permanent form of thanks and remembrance: They made the Sego Lily the state flower of Utah.

Not as common as the white Sego is the yellow Sego. Once, the Sego Lily and its cousin the orange Desert Mariposa Lily, grew in great patches, even fields, in the deserts and on desert slopes. Now I find them mostly as solitary plants in unexpected places. Riding jauntily atop slender, flexible stems, Sego and Mariposa lilies are easy to remember. They nod as you walk by.

Solitary plants struggling to survive are a common sight in the Great Basin Desert. It is a lonely place, that section of country that would be split by the boundary line between Utah and Nevada if such lines were more than a mapmaker's convenience. Few people, fewer towns. If the Great Basin Desert were the Arabian Desert this section would be the Empty Quarter.

Once, I sat for lunch in the sketchy shade of Big Sagebrush on the Nevada side. An apple, raisins, a thick slice of sourdough bread, and a flask of water. Solitary meals in lonesome places stimulate reveries. My thoughts turned to the evocation of American wildflowers in song, prose and poetry. To my surprise, most of my recollections were of general, although lyrical, descriptions of wildflowers. Robert Frost found a "leaping tongue of bloom" that had been spared by the scythe but he does not tell us what flower it is. William Cullen Bryant's unnamed prairie wildflowers are so numerous as to "rival the constellations." The 1927 recording of "Wildwood Flower" by the original Carter Family is a song of all wildflowers that defined the idiom of American mountain folk music.

Lilacs are a favorite of poets, but they are garden flowers. Amy Lowell's lilacs "watching a deserted house," and Walt Whitman's "lilacs last in the **SAGEBRUSH** doorway bloomed," are, we suspect, garden lilacs gone wild. In fact, the Lilac Sunbonnet, one of a few wildflowers of the West bearing a lilac name, is not a lilac at all; it is the Spotted Langloisia, and it gets its popular name from the lilac color of its flower. John Greenleaf Whittier told us all we need to know of the goldenrod when he explained why the flowers sag from their stems. Goldenrods droop, he wrote, because they are "heavy with sunshine." Elinor Wylie drew a sensuous image when she proposed that she and her lover go from the city and "live among wild peaches." Few fruits have a more beautiful bloom than the peach. Fewer still are those who know where the wild peach grows. The desert, however, produces a wild peach, a small, thorny shrub or tree with pink blossoms and bitter fruit. A springtime search may turn up a Desert Peach and its sister, the white-flowered Desert Apricot.

No prose, poetry, or song that I could recall that day in the sagebrush was alone responsible for popular recognition of an American wildflower. But I had been guilty of a student's

The cowboy, first and foremost in the gallery of American heroes, did much of his riding, roping and branding while surrounded by Sagebrush, ARTEMESIA spp., Many of the expansive cattle ranges of the Great Basin were in the "Sagebrush Desert," so-named because the woody Sagebrushes dominate plant life. The cowboy of the Old West has ridden off into the sunset. On his last ride, surely, he guided his mustang through great patches of Big Sagebrush, ARTEMESIA TRIDENTATA, Black Sagebrush, A. ARBUSCULA, and the other range sagebrushes.

habit of consulting my memory instead of reading the landscape before me. A short walk from my Sagebrush shelter brought me face-to-face with a scattered growth of Desert Sage, or Purple Sage, the purple-bracted, silver-leaved plant that Zane Grey made famous in his 1910 novel, "Riders of the Purple Sage."

Purple Sage is a low and spreading plant, beautiful without ostentation in its lance-shaped leaves and its small, clustered blue flowers subtended by purple bracts. Counter to popular belief, it is not a variety of Sagebrush. Like a little sister, Purple Sage tags along with Sagebrush over much of the Great Basin. Find big brother and little sister is usually nearby. Zane Grey's novel and the motion pictures it inspired were so enfolded into the American imagination that they nearly turned Purple Sage into the national flower, even though few Americans have ever actually seen a Purple Sage.

Our cinematic vision of the American West does not include cowboys riding through fields of flowers, purple or otherwise. Zane Grey, the logic goes, must have meant Sagebrush. Cowboys, everybody knows, ride through thorny, clawing brush — Sagebrush and Chaparral. Otherwise, why would cowboys wear those ridiculous, flapping, leather chaps? Flowers, indeed! But, there is no denying it — Purple Sage is a flower, an herb, a soft-stemmed plant that dies and regenerates annually. Sagebrush, on the other hand, is a woody shrub of indeterminate life. Zane Grey (1872-1939) made the Purple Sage and the color purple, wherever either appears, as defining the mood or the ambience of the Great Basin Desert. The word "purple" appears about once in every ten pages of the novel. But the reader probably can't describe it, except as it blooms in the imagination.

Mountain men as well as cowboys were savvy about the desert's secrets for survival. Jedediah Strong Smith, Bible-toting mountain man, and Christopher Houston Carson, eagle-eyed Western scout, journeyed across the Great Basin Desert at a time in American history when there were no wheels west of the Rocky Mountains. Old Jedediah crossed "the plains of sand" from California to Salt Lake in 1827. Two years later, Kit Carson, then a scout for Explorer John Charles Fremont, took a party of men through the Great Basin from Salt Lake to California. Unaware of Jedediah's earlier march, Carson wrote that the desert "had

The fragrance of Sage, wafting in from mountain canyons on rainy nights, was one of the many elements that made up the menacing-

SAGE

narcissistic atmosphere of Raymond Chandler's tough detective novels set in Los Angeles. Not only in Los Angeles, but throughout the West, many species of Sage add diversity to desert plant life. One of the most useful sages to the American Indian was blue-flowered Chia, SALVIA spp. From Chia seed, the Indians made pinole, a staple of their diets.

never before been crossed by white men." Jedediah later noted merely that he had made the journey. Carson wrote of the crossing as if it had been little more trying than a stroll to town. But an eyewitness described the arrival of Carson's party at Sutter's Fort as a band of skeleton men leading a herd of skeleton mules.

Mountain men like Smith and Carson learned to live off the land. It was often a condition of survival. On trapping, trading and exploring expeditions they carried a minimum amount of such necessities as salt, flour, and coffee. Coffee, in particular, was relished by the Indians, who called it the White Man's "black medicine." Without coffee before the traders came, the Indians, nevertheless, had several hot drinks they brewed from plants. The most popular and best-known of these was Squaw Tea, a name used for both the plant and the beverage. Indians, Mexicans, and old-timers made Ephedra Tea by boiling a handful of twigs in water. The desert Indians, without metal utensils before arrival of the Spanish, brewed Ephedra Tea by dropping hot stones into closely woven baskets filled with water.

Ephedra, EPHEDRA spp., is a green plant that appears to be composed of closely-packed, leafless stems. A close look reveals the tiny, scale-like leaves of the plant. The plants bear tiny fruits, like miniature pine cones. When Ephedra plants reach maturity, about four feet high, they have a windswept appearance that is usually associated with plants of the seashore.

I cannot confirm that the mountain men enjoyed Squaw **SQUAW TEA** Tea when they ran short of coffee but logic tells me that they did since it was a favored drink — under many different names — throughout the desert West and Southwest. On the other hand, another desert traveler, Horace Greeley, was no live-off-the-land beaver trapper. He was an imperious editor and politician. Greeley, one would expect, demanded his Select Darjeeling Blend, even when his stagecoach made a stop at Simpson's Spring in the Great Basin Desert.

Squaw Tea of the Old West is one of the truly peculiar plants of the desert. Its names are as numerous as its peculiarities. The plant is also known as Mexican Tea, Mormon Tea, Joint Fir, Joint Pine, Drovers Tea, Indian Tea, Desert Tea, Teamsters Tea, Brigham Tea, and, most likely, other names I have never heard. The many names for the plant and the tea made from Ephedra are an indication of its widespread acceptance in the West. A close examination of Ephreda, a many-branched shrub with jointed stems, discloses the startling fact that it is a conifer. When the plant is in full flower, bearing beautiful catkins, the male cone, resembling a miniature pine cone, is covered with pollen. The cone of the female plant contains a pair of achenes (naked

seeds). The names Joint Pine and Joint Fir are attributed to the cones surprisingly found on this little plant. It gains the adjective "joint" because the stems are jointed and break easily and cleanly at the joints. Usually, the stems are swollen with spindle-shaped nodes, the work of a gall wasp.

After setting up camp one desert evening, I walked a short distance down a dry wash in search of Ephedra. Before I spotted the shrub, I was startled to find several Desert or Apache Plumes in full flower. It is no exaggeration to use the verb "startled" in describing the first Desert Plume of the wildflower season. The lovely flower is so unlike most other desert flowers that it earns the verb.

Desert Plume's first distinction is that, unlike most desert wildflowers, it is usually taller than the sagebrush or other shrubs growing in the same area. (Some desert flowers go to the opposite extreme — the plants lie supine on the desert floor. The blooms are so tiny that the flower hunter must recline to see them; hence the generic name, "belly flowers.") Desert Plume's tall plumes of yellow flowers are so regal in the desert setting that it was surely necessary for some romantic to attribute royalty to them. And that was done with one of the plant's popular names, Golden Prince's Plume. To me, though, when I see Desert Plume's feathery outline from some distance I am reminded of Old Ben Franklin's quill pens.

Back in camp with a handful of Ephedra stems, I dropped them in a pot of boiling water and left them to steep while I heated up frijoles con toro and corn tortillas. I sat with my back to a sun-warmed boulder and watched the setting sun redden the sky behind distant mountains. A rich, spicy aroma arose from my mug of Squaw Tea. I sipped slowly, wondering if — like thousands of Indians, Spaniards, Mexicans, and Westerners before me — I was drinking the very essence of the desert. And as I sat on the desert floor in a patch of low-growing plants bearing closed buds, the sun began its descent, a journey that would take the sun's lifegiving light and warmth to another distant landscape. The plants around me were clumps of Dune Evening Primrose, and their tightly-wound buds were poised for one of nature's unusual performances.

In the dance of the Dune Evening Primrose, the setting sun had an important role.

Paiute Cabbage was an old, Western name for Prince's Plume because Indians boiled young leaves of the plant. They made for a tasty potherb. That, however, **PRINCE'S PLUME** *would be a dangerous idea for today's cooks. Prince's Plume, STANLEYA PINNATA, contains toxic selenium. The plant must be boiled in several changes of water. However, selenium content does not detract from the majestic beauty of the yellow flowers at the tip of five-foot stalks.*

DUNE EVENING PRIMROSE

Like an abandoned bridal bouquet, the Dune Evening Primrose, OENOTHERA DELTOIDES, *blooms in white profusion upon the quiet desert sands. At eventide, as if synchronized by an enchanted choreographer, thousands of white flowers unfurl in an explosion of delicate, white petals. But for this "Cinderella" flower life is but a fleeting moment, for by mid-morning of the next day its loveliness has wilted away. The splendor of the evening is well spent. The sweetness of its perfume spills upon the air intoxicating Hawkmoths and other flying insects who come to drink of its nectar and help pollinate the plant. After the party is over, and before the stroke of mid-day, bees come to clean up after the party, collecting any pollen left upon the petals.*

It played the part that dimming house lights play in a theater production. As the sunlight faded, the primrose buds began their synchronized performance. At the tip of the buds, the lobes slowly parted, showing a trace of white. Then faster. The white petals appeared and with a single motion the petals unfurled and dropped into place, freeing the yellow, pollen-saturated anthers at the center. Across the sandy wash the plain plants of a few seconds before had become decorated with the ghostly white flowers of the Dune Evening Primrose. The silken, five-petaled flowers of the primrose remain open during the night — silvery beacons that announce themselves as feeding stations to the flying and crawling insects of the desert. The hungry insects of the night reward the primroses that provide their midnight meals. The insects carry the flower's sticky pollen from plant to plant.

DUNE EVENING PRIMROSE

Dune Evening Primrose, OENOTHERA DELTOIDES, is a plant of many names: Desert Primrose, Devils Lantern, Lion-in-a-Cage, Birdcage Primrose, and Fairy Basket. The last four names describe the dead and dried plant as it has appeared to various observers. Desert lore warns that the Sidewinder likes to lurk in the coarse stems and leaves of the primrose. The Sidewinder is a small rattlesnake that strikes without activating its warning buzzer.

The Dune Primrose shows two faces. One, of course, is blossom time when the flowers may cover large areas of the desert. The second persona of the Dune Evening Primrose begins with the annual death of the plants. As the plant dies and turns brown, the prostrate branches curl upward over the main, woody stem. In that dying and dead stage the plant shapes itself into a birdcage. It is always surprising to walk into a patch of perfectly-formed, natural birdcages in the wilderness. As might be expected, that reconstitution in death gives the flower its popular name, "Birdcage Primrose." I once met a gray-haired lady kneeling before a Birdcage, which she studied with a wistful smile. She told me they were "Fairy Baskets made by Primrose," and she had loved them from childhood. I said yes they are nice but around here we call them Birdcages, not Fairy Baskets. She nailed me with a withering look that ended the conversation and surely, forevermore, banished the heresy of my name for her Fairy Baskets.

The deserts are home to dozens of white flowers, in addition to the white flowers of the Primrose, the deadly Jimson Weed and Prickly Poppy. My reaction to the first white flowers I encountered on desert trails was a question: Why do white flowers, and other white objects, seem whiter on the desert than elsewhere?

The answer to that question is uncomplicated.

Whiteness is a measure of the amount of the sun's rays reflected by an object. In clear desert air, more of the sun's rays reach the earth's surface, giving objects more rays to reflect. So white is whiter. Sometimes so white that it appears to be day-glow white. Once I was detracted from my purpose by a white flower. I was searching a jumble of tub-sized boulders, hoping to see a chunky, slow-moving Chuckwalla that had been reported in the neighborhood. Walking around a boulder I came upon a flowering Desert Chicory that had somehow found a home in a sliver of earth between boulders. The notched-petal flowers were so bright white in the desert sunshine that they held my attention for a minute. Then, from the corner of an eye, I saw a big, fat tail disappear over a boulder. My Chuckwalla, almost certainly. But I never saw the rest of that foot-long lizard.

The lovely, white petaled Desert Chicory, RAFINESQUIA NEOMEXICANA, *is just one of the plants that can be found in many of the American deserts.*

DESERT CHICORY

Another white flower of exceptional beauty is the Desert Star. After a winter when nature has provided plentiful showers, the white-flowered Desert Star, reacts with enthusiasm. The little plant produces so many flowers in a mounded cluster that it resembles the neat small bouquets that bridesmaids carry. Flowers of the desert star — white rays with a yellow center — are normally the width of a thumb. But I remember one dry year when I hunted in vain for Desert Stars until I realized I had walked by a dozen or more plants. That year the Desert Stars had used all their stored, but reduced, energy to produce only one or two larger white flowers on each plant.

The white, night blooming plant with the tantalizing name Queen of the Night is certain to arouse anyone's curiosity. After I had found a Queen of the Night, listed in field guides as Night Blooming Cereus, my curiosity was greater than ever. Its many-petaled, white flowers are the width of a palm. That large size makes them conspicuous in the desert. But even at fairly close range, the lovely, sweet-scented flowers appeared to be growing on a dead bush. A closer examination shows that the Night-Blooming Cereus is a gray cactus, with many sparsely-spined, twig-like stems. None of those features, though, explain the Lady of the Night name. That comes from its flowering regimen: the flowers open in late evening or night and close in early morning. Its red fruit, by the way, is one of the many cactus fruits eaten by Indians of the Southwest.

Not all plants have names that ring poetic like the Queen of the Night, or Desert

Star, but are named because of peculiar characteristics. The Mule's Ears is one such flower. Most everything about a mule is distinctive. The mule's powerful kick is legendary. The mule is born with a disposition that switches back and forth between mean, ornery, cantankerous and vicious. Especially distinctive are the mule's long, pointed ears — which the mule manipulates as if they were rooted in swivels. Some teamster of the long-ago Southwest — driver of a team of mules or horses, or a span of oxen — looked at a desert plant with long, resinous leaves and was reminded of the ears of a mule. "Them's like Mule's Ears," he said, and the name stuck.

The lanceolate leaves of the Mule's Ears plant are as much as two feet long. They are shiny as if they had been brushed with varnish. Growing from the Mule's Ears clumps are long stalks. The big, yellow flowers, with yellow centers, grow at **MULE'S EARS** the end of the stalks. The flowers are as big as a man's fist, and are made up of as many as two dozen rays.

Mules fascinate. In a time of war in a land called Burma I walked on a slippery jungle trail with a column of warriors known as the Mars Task Force. Sure-footed mules were the transportation of choice in that treacherous terrain. Muleskinners, some thought, had an unfair advantage. Going uphill a muleskinner could hang onto the mule's tail. Ski along on the mud under mule-power. Curious, I put some questions to Lt. Martin Thrailkill of Texas, the head muleskinner of the outfit. I asked him what makes a good muleskinner. "To start with," Thrailkill said, "he should have as much sense as the mule." It was not a disparagement of soldiers. It was a compliment to the animal that carried mortars, rations and medicines where no wheels could go. Hopefully some day, someone will name a sturdy plant after this valiant animal — after the entire mule, not just his ears.

Desert old-timers gave names of familiar things to the new plants they encountered while crossing the deserts. Mule's Ears, WYETHIA AMPLEXICAULIS, is named for the appearance of the long, leaves of this plant. Jackass Clover, Horsebush, and Horsenettle were named for these working animals. Rattlesnake Weed and Snakehead were named for their similarity in color to those serpents. Buffalo and Coyote were thought to be fond of Buffalo Gourd and Coyote Gourd, Even the lowly flea was remembered in the name Fleabane.

"But it's not as pretty as a Texas Bluebonnet."

That line was a family joke, as well as a tribute to the best-known flower of the Lone Star State. It was the product of my grandmother's infatuation with the Texas Bluebonnet. My grandparents, Newt and Phoebe Crumpler of Boone County, Arkansas, left their home on Bear Creek in the Ozark Mountains in 1899 to visit Texas. Grandpa had heard that good grazing land was available in the Big Bend country of West Texas. They decided to go see for themselves.

The Texas Bluebonnet, LUPINUS SUBCARNOSUS, a lupine that is native to the **BLUEBONNET** *Big Bend country, stands three or four feet tall on a single stem, a wand that carries clusters of blue flowers with white centers. The Bluebonnet's leaflets radiate from the end of stems, like the spokes in a wheel.*

They loaded the family in a covered wagon, a Springfield wagon. The wagon cargo included bedclothes, cooking utensils, and rations — everything needed for a long trip. They drove 25 miles over the rough mountain trails to the railroad station at Cricket, Arkansas. At Cricket, Grandpa drove the wagon and team onto a flatbed railroad car that he had hired. The family and horses camped out on the flatbed until steam locomotives of the freight train landed them in Texas. The Big Bend country of the Rio Grande River was a land in ferment that year. Ranchers, settlers, Mexicans, and Indians rode through a land the Mexicans called El Despoblado, "the empty country."

Grandpa drove the team about 15 miles a day. Every night the family gathered around a campfire there on the empty country of the Chihuahuan Desert for the big meal of the day. But Grandpa didn't like the desert. They drove back to the railhead, hired another flatbed rail car and returned to the Arkansas Ozarks the same way they had come — sightseers on their own private railroad car.

It must have been a great adventure. But when people asked Grandma about the trip, she wanted to talk about Texas Bluebonnets. "Beautiful Texas Bluebonnets, they grow from the edge of the road clear out to the end of the world," Grandma said. She was not normally guilty of hyperbole like that, but Texas Bluebonnets seemed to have lodged themselves in her very soul.

Whenever the beauty of an Arkansas flower — cultured in the garden or wild in the woods — was mentioned to Grandma, her response was always "But it's not as pretty as a Texas Bluebonnet." That went on for several years, until the family, anticipating Grandma's next line, beat her to the chorus: "But it's not as pretty as a Texas Bluebonnet."

No wonder Grandma got carried away. In good years, the Bluebonnets, state flower of Texas, lay out wide carpets of blue and white in great areas of "the empty country."

On one spring day in the desert my Grandma's words were put to a challenge when I came across a boulevard bordered with flowers. What hero was this place made for, I wondered. Where is the victorious army? Where are the silver-**LUPINE** caparisoned steeds, the ivory-trimmed chariots, the rebellious queen in gold chains?

No hand of man made that Way of The Triumphant. Water in sheets had flowed straight as a crossbowman's arrow, scouring a boulevard into the desert floor and endowing it with curbs of gravel. Not gravel of emeralds or turquoise, I will stipulate, except when the sun captured the green of cactus and the blue of the sky and carried them to the sands.

Blue flowers lined the way in ranks as true as if they had been planted by a gardener with a chalk line. Blue flowers of **DESERT MARIGOLD** the Lupine as blue as the Odyssean seas, danced away into the distance. Clusters of the Lupine flowers at the tip of the plant's spears stood at solemn attention. The petals opened wide to show a golden throat. A kiss for the victors? Rich green leaves of the Lupine imitated the form of chariot wheels.

The land was quiet, the boulevard deserted. I squared my shoulders and sucked in my stomach. I lifted my chin. I marched down the boulevard between the rows of blue Lupine, swinging my walking staff, wondering what I would find at the other end.

"Pea Flowers" is a common country name for the blue and lilac-blue flowers of the Lupine, LUPINUS spp. The Lupines are members of the pea family. Texans assure us that the Bluebonnet, Texas state flower, possesses a beauty found in no other Lupine. Often Lupines mingle with Desert Marigolds and weave brilliant blue and yellow blankets on the desert floor.

Yes, I have seen the Yellow Brick Road. It sometimes appears on the desert floor when spring rains bring a profusion of Desert Marigolds, BAILEYA MULTIRADIATA, on a gravel bar or a strip of sand. The golden yellows of this and related flowers are so intense that some long-ago, anonymous flower lover named it to honor the Virgin Mary: Mary's Gold, consolidated in time to Marigold.

Deserts as large as the Chihuahuan are home to much more than an imagined Carthaginian road. Especially spectactular in the Chihuahuan Desert are its many cactus plants. There is hardly a cactus that does not claim some unusual feature or behavioral characteristic.

The Horse-Crippler Cactus sits so low on the ground that horses do not always see it. They can be crippled by stepping on the plant and its stout spines. The Claret Cup Cactus likes high, rocky places. It is a big, spreading cactus that produces many flowers from a mounded clump of plants. The fruit, tuna, is red and plump. From that environment the plant gives birth to flowers of dazzling scarlet. It is the red of Marilyn Monroe's lipstick.

The Rainbow Cactus is a cactus that gets its name from the bands of colored spines that circle its short, cylindrical body. The fruit is green. Half-inch spines are white, pink, gray, and yellow. Bathed in sunlight, this cactus is truly a desert rainbow. Rainbow Cactus is sparing in its production of pink, rose, lavender **CLARET CUP** or yellow flowers. Often only one flower, but it can produce a few more. Yellow, the yellow of just-churned butter, is my favorite flower of the Rainbow Cactus.

Cactus erupts with flower colors for every personality — a butter-yellow for epicures, and a lipstick red for libertines. Ah, the force we call nature. Its wonders are endless.

Don't dig up a Blackfoot Daisy looking for a root shaped like a pair of Nikes at midnight. Somehow this bushy plant of the desert got stuck with a Latin name meaning "black foot," but no one knows why. The flower grows from rusty stems on a dark green plant that is low and rounded. The flowers have notched petals that radiate from a dull yellow button. Don't look for bright colors on the Blackfoot Daisy either.

The flowers of the Rainbow Cactus, ECHINOCEREUS DASYACANTHUS display a range of rainbow colors. They can be yellow, pink, rose, or lavender. But its name comes from the bands of delicately colored spines -- pink, yellow, brown, gray, or **RAINBOW CACTUS** *white -- that girdle the plant. It is a tiny, squat cactus -- from four to twelve inches tall. When the big, cup-shaped flower appears, the plant looks top-heavy.*

The Chihuahuan Desert of the United States covers portions of Texas, New Mexico and Arizona. It is noted for its many flowering cactus plants and for a panorama of unusual plants. Among the cacti is the Claret Cup Cactus, ECHINOCEREUS TRIGLOCHIDIATUS.

More than a thousand species of cacti have been identified on the seven continents. These strange-looking plants

CLARET CUP

have been used to make candy, preserves, beer, and strong liquor. The strong internal structures of dead cactus are used for building material. Luther Burbank selected a cactus for use as cattle feed. Of the many species, the most widespread and best-known is the Prickly Pear,

OPUNTIA spp. But the most spectacular cactus flower appears on the Claret Cup Cactus, ECHINOCEREUS TRIGLOCHIDIATUS. Two-inch scarlet flowers bloom on spiny stems. They are the shape and depth of a tea cup, adding an unusual dimension to the flower. Bigger and older plants grow enormous clusters of Claret Cup flowers -- sometimes turning a desert hillside into an alfresco flower show of startling beauty.

It is off-white, maybe tattletale gray, and likes rocky places at the edge of desert washes.

Another desert dweller that prefers sandy washes is the Harvester Ant and I came across one of their colonies not far from the Blackfoot Daisy. A troupe of Harvester Ants came marching by while I sat in a spot of shade. The big, red ants lock-stepped across the sand as if they had elected me as their reviewing officer. Every soldier carried a tiny sheet of foliage — like a green banner of defiance against lizards, those marauding dinosaurs of the ant world. The ants marched straight and true to their ant dome on the sand. The center of the dome was the entrance to the underground kingdom of the Harvester Ants. The entrance was a hole about the size of a 25-cent coin. Sloping outward in a circle is the evacuated dirt and sand, and the debris of ant civilization, carried out by the soldiers and spread evenly from the entrance. Ants are picky old maids, everything has to be apple-pie neat. That dome was about two feet in circumference, and an inch high at the entrance.

I waved goodbye to the Harvester Ants. They continued marching as if my departure was an event they could take or leave. Farther up the wash I found a Woolly Marigold which, like the Blackfoot Daisy, is another member of the Sunflower family. The Desert Marigold flower, however, is brilliant yellow with a yellow button. The plant itself is woolly and gray-white, and seldom grows above knee-high. I like the Woolly Marigold's many-petaled, notched flowers. As many as forty petals radiate from the center, bestowing a full, rich appearance upon the flower.

Well, another band of ants marched under the Woolly Marigold and made a sharp left at the second flower. Like you and me marching under a flower the size of the Superdome. I continued my walk along the trace of the Butterfield Overland Mail Company through a little desert valley hemmed in by low, rocky hills. It had been more than 130 years since the stagecoaches had rumbled through the Southwestern desert from St. Louis to San Francisco. Any passenger who had come this far on the stagecoach, I thought, must have been black and

Blackfoot Daisy, MELAMPODIUM LEUCANTHUM, grows as a rounded bush, reaching a height of nearly two feet. The flowers, which can bloom for as much as eight months of the year -- March to November -- like rocky parts of the desert. Up to ten white rays radiate from a yellow button.

BLACKFOOT DAISY

The Woolly Marigold, BAILEYA PLENIRADIATA, is one of a family of plants that are sometimes classified as "Woolly Sunflowers." They include the Woolly Marigold, the Sneezeweeds and the Goldfields. All are members of the Sunflower tribe and all are covered with woolly hairs. The Woolly Marigold is covered all over with white hairs. The flower has as many as 40 yellow rays growing from a yellow button.

WOOLLY MARIGOLD

blue from the ride. The 2,800-mile journey through desert and mountain followed a trail that was little more than the wheel ruts laid down by the previous stagecoach. Old John Butterfield might have made a success of the 25-day schedule from St. Louis to San Francisco if the Civil War had not halted all transportation that crossed the new, uncharted boundaries between North and South.

Pulled by the magnet of a splash of green in that dry valley, I crossed to the other side. As I walked nearer, the green turned into a patch of Cola de Mico, a Spanish name meaning "Monkey Tail." It is commonly known as Quail Plant or Sand Heliotrope, and that patch lived up to the name. A dozen plump quail ran from the protection of the knee-high creepers that make up Cola de Mico. The quail ran to the hill and the protection of the boulders, black plumes riding high atop rusty-red heads.

Blue-green Cola de Mico is distinguished by coiled pairs of tiny white or lavender flowers. It is the coiled branches that give this plant its "Monkey Tail" name. Quail feed on the seeds and find protection in this low-growing plant. I have also flushed jackrabbits from Cola de Mico, which provides both forage and cover for the **HELIOTROPE** long-eared, black-tailed hares.

I finished crossing the valley by walking to the hillside boulders where I had seen the quail disappear. Not in pursuit of the quail, but for a pleasant spot to take a late afternoon rest-break. I found a Heliotrope in full flower, and sat on a flat-topped boulder close by. This variety is called Fragrant or Sweet-Scented Heliotrope. From my granite stool I enjoyed its pleasant scent. Both Cola de Mico and Heliotrope plants are inclined toward a sprawling posture. One-inch, grayish-white with yellow centers —shaped like inch-wide funnels — grew at the tips of coiled stems of the Heliotrope. The flower is one of those that curls up against the hot sun, and opens in the cooler hours of the evening.

As I left the lair of the Heliotrope, I heard the reunion calls of the quail family coming from scattered parts of the hillside — a sure signal that sundown was near and bedtime was approaching for the desert quail.

Not all plants are large enough to provide refuge for desert creatures nor display spectacular blooms. Not much to look at, the sparsely-leaved Vervain is nonetheless a flower to

Heliotrope, HELIOTROPIUM CONVOLVULACEUM, has a pleasant fragrance, hard to describe. Western pioneers, though, gave it a name fresh from ranch house kitchens, "Cherry Pie Flower." That identified the fragrance and gave an original American name to a wild plant that is familiar in European and South American gardens.

reckon with in any serious discussion of man's interrelationships with the plant world. Don't believe it? Then consider this: In 1957 I crossed the desert from Amman with a colonel of the Jordan Arab Legion. He stopped in a patch of Vervain less than half a day's journey from Jerusalem. The colonel lightly flicked a Vervain spike with his swagger stick. "Did you know this is a holy plant?" he said. "It is the plant that was used to stop the bleeding of Christ. After he was taken down from the Crucifixion."

Well, later I looked it up. Herb-of-the-Cross was the common name for Vervain in English-speaking Europe and the Biblical East. The state flower of New Mexico, Vervain, common throughout the deserts of the Southwest, is less than noble in appearance. It is a small, pink, five-petaled flower growing on the erect spikes of the plant. The color of the flower ranges from lavender to blue. The plant is covered with hairs.

One Vervain name, Pigeon's Grass, comes down from the time when wild pigeons darkened the skies. But all seed-eating songbirds, not just pigeons, feast on the seeds of Vervain. Bird lovers plant Vervain in the garden and watch the acrobatics as birds cling to the spikes to harvest the seeds.

Birds are a common sighting in the desert. Many birds depend upon the desert's bounty for food and shelter. As I walked along a **VERVAIN** gently-sloping sand wash dotted with Creosote Bush, Desert Willow, and Catsclaw, I turned into a little canyon. I searched for noonday shade from the hot desert sun and found it under a perpendicular rock bluff that formed a jutting awning over a little patch of sand. A great place for lunch. Even better than I had expected because a pair of hawks soared high over the canyon. Too high to identify, but most likely two Red-tails.

After a lunch of cheese, apple, and cold tea, I walked on up the canyon. It was a short walk. The canyon ended abruptly in a tangle of boulders scattered at the foot of another rock wall. Spreading among the rocks was a big patch of Rock Nettle in full bloom. The creamy, two-inch flowers were so profuse that they seemed intent on hiding the dark green foliage of the plant. Rock Nettle is one of the many plants that are commonly given the generic name, "Stinging Nettle." Stingers they are, too. The Rock Nettle delivers a vicious sting to the unwary who would rob the

FLOWER GARDEN

Painters who work from nature have an advantage over studio artists in one respect demonstrated by this photograph of Curled Nama, NAMA HISPIDUM, Woolly Marigold, BAILEYA PLENIRADIATA, and Spine Aster, MACHAERANTHERA sp. That advantage is composition -- nature has already composed the perfect picture.

Following page: Vervain's, VERBENA spp., usefulness in healing is widely known. Around the world it is believed to be the plant used to staunch the flowing blood of the crucified Christ, hence its name, Herb-of-the-Cross.

plant of its five-petaled blossoms. The color of the flowers, incidentally, may be either cream or yellow. Stinging Nettle was once a common green vegetable in Europe. (Boiling the plant removed the chemicals that cause stinging.) American Indians laid out (carefully!) stalks of Stinging Nettle. The plant material rotted and left linen-like fibers, which Indian women used to make cloth.

The inventiveness of folk doctors knows no limits. An old granny remedy for arthritis was to flagellate the patient's skin at the offending joints. The flagellum was Stinging Nettle. The patient instantly felt intense, burning pain and witnessed — perhaps with some alarm — appearance of a skin rash. The pain and the rash, so believers said, sucked the pain from the joints. Ouch!

Many folk remedies seemed pretty hostile treatment for the poor patient. The desert too, at first glance, is a harsh and hostile place, a blistering emptiness, an unfinished part of the earth. Even its color, the neutrality of faded gray or tan, predicts a barren and wasted land. But when I walk into the desert, eyes open and all senses alert, the timeless land becomes a world of revealed wonders. The somber, earthen pastel of the landscape is the

Five-petaled Rock Nettle,
EUCNIDE RUPESTRIS, grows well in
the rocky ledges **WARNOCK'S ROCK NETTLE** flawless backdrop for the spots of color that are ever in the
along the Rio Grande River. desert, waiting to be disclosed to the seeking eye.
Parts of the plant were used by
Indians to make a green dye.

I had walked up a desert dry wash for half an hour and had seen little color other than the many-hued greens of hot-country shrubs. I circled a mesquite hoping to find something of interest on the other side. My reward was an explosion of color. A solitary Desert or Mojave Aster bush, its magnificent flowers in full bloom, flourished alone by a dirt bank of the wash. It is hyperbole, of course, to say that a single blooming Desert Aster plant is an "explosion of color." But the somber desert does that to one's senses. The desert magnifies and intensifies everything within its authority.

The purple and yellow flowers of the Desert Aster dominated the dry wash at that moment. After I had marveled — for the hundredth time with a hundred flowers — at the miracle of the flower's architecture and color, I turned and walked away. I looked back. The Desert Aster was still there, a small but resplendent oasis of beauty. It was not a mirage.

flowers
Painted
Desert

A cool, refreshing breeze blew steadily through the little pass in the high desert where I walked on a hot August day. The breeze was created because the cooler air of the high desert rushed in like water running downhill, to fill the dryer, hotter space of the desert below. Steady, near-constant breezes are a feature of the high desert. The most picturesque and striking of our high deserts is the Painted Desert of New Mexico, Arizona and Utah.

The physical beauty of the Painted Desert is so overwhelming that it diminishes everything else of man and nature. Even wildflowers seem less bright among the multi-hued castles, turrets, flying buttresses, arches, and gargoyles carved from the standing stone by wind and water. Above all, the Painted Desert is Indian country, homeland of the Navaho and Hopi. The steppe-desert topography and plant life combine with the timeless cultures of the Navaho and Hopi to make the Painted Desert one of the last bastions of the ancient lifestyle of the "gatherer."

"Gatherer" is one of the terms anthropologists use to classify peoples according to the principal methods they use to obtain food. Other classifications include "hunter" and "cultivator." In the Painted Desert, Native Americans "gather" energy-rich nuts, fruit of the pinyon pine tree, in the same manner as their ancestors. Collection of pinyon nuts is an annual autumn outing for many Native families. Harvesting is an uncomplicated business. The spiny, green cones — about the size of a tennis ball — are knocked from the ends of crooked, arthritic branches with long, hooked poles. Athletic children scramble among the trees like Fox Squirrels to dislodge pinyon cones in difficult to reach areas. The harvesters toss the cones into campfires. The heat opens the cones with a pop. The pine nut gatherers then rake the cones from the fire and pick out the fruit. Every cone contains about half a dozen rich, brown nuts (piñones in Spanish).

Windblown seeds of desert plants find shelter in unusual places. When a seed lodges in friendly territory — JUNIPER *be it the crack of a rock, a trailside ditch or between fallen tree limbs — the seed will produce another plant. In a desert, where such lodgings are few, seeds seek out every natural haven, even these snarled Juniper, JUNIPERUS sp. logs.*

Like other nuts, pinyon nuts can be eaten raw. And like other nuts, their flavor is improved by roasting. Still, it must be said that a lunch of just-picked pine nuts is one of the great pleasures available to the high desert walker. Throughout the Southwest, pinyon nuts are a basic commodity in the pantry of good cooks. They are sold in food stores and are the most important nut crop from trees that are not grown commercially. It is interesting to note that Native Americans, who do not believe in private ownership of trees or other things produced by nature, have a special dispensation for pinyon trees. The harvesting rights to certain pinyon pines are allotted to particular Indian families or clans — not as ownership, but as a courtesy based on long traditions of use by that family.

I remember an unexpected discovery on a crisp autumn day in another pinyon pine area. The biggest of the pinyon pines, a tree that had provided perhaps 300 years of harvests for hungry Native Americans, showed signs of decline. **PINYON PINE** With the death and decay of limbs and branches, the pinyon's foliage had become more open and airy. Drought, disease, and the work of insects had hollowed the trunk. The hollow trunk could no longer circulate sap and was under a sentence of death. But even as the pinyon faced slow death, it had become a city, a factory, and a nursery for a swarm of wild honeybees.

While I watched, worker bees flew to the tree from the flower pastures of the desert. The nectar-carrying workers flew straight to a knothole in the trunk, and disappeared into a hidden kingdom of pollen, honey, wax and larvae. The robbing of bee-trees is a fine art with Native Americans. They stun the bees with smoke, then remove sections of honey-dripping cone. But Indians always leave enough comb to assure that the honey-making and bee-producing life cycle of the honeybees continues.

I stopped on my walk among the pines to admire a juniper. It was loaded with the silvery-white berries that make the tree resemble a Christmas tree decorated with miniature, metallic bulbs. Pinyon and juniper are so closely associated that botanists refer to "the pinyon-juniper woodland communities" of the American Southwest. As conifers go, both pinyon and juniper are short trees, seldom exceeding 35 feet in height.

Rugged Pinyon Pine, PINUS sp., trees are tough enough to survive on the cold, high mesas of Navajo country in the Painted Desert. Environmental conditions may turn them into twisted, dwarf trees that would not be out of place in a Japanese garden. Help in reproduction is provided by the Pinyon Jay, a bird that flies away with a beakful of pinyon nuts and always drops a few.

At the peak of its beauty, Indian Paintbrush, CASTILLEJA *sp.*, seems to be beckoning, demanding the attention of everything in its domain. The name itself — Indian Paintbrush — comes close to describing its appearance. The colors — orange, red, yellow — might be the colors in an Indian blanket or basket, even war paint. The plume shape could be that of a single feather in the headband of a

INDIAN PAINTBRUSH

hunting warrior. Or a colorful ornament in the glistening ebony hair of a shy Indian maiden. Indian Paintbrush deserves the attention it claims for its vivid colors and its stand-straight posture.

Juniper has a special use for the Navajo of the Painted Desert. The *shaman* directing the War Dance — part of the ceremonies to drive out evil spirits that have made a Navajo ill — supervises the building of a great arbor made of juniper boughs. In this brush shelter, the Navajos entertain the guests they have invited to the War Dance.

All three of these food bounties of nature — pinyon nuts, wild honey, and juniper berries — were gathered by Native Americans. But they had to "get there first." Squirrels, rodents, and other small mammals feast on pinyon nuts. Native peoples ate juniper berries either fresh or cooked in cakes. But birds dine on the berries straight off the tree. Bears ignore the sting of bees while raiding bee-trees, lapping up every drop of honey, and eating the larvae.

It was early morning — my shadow was still long. I walked along a dry wash that supported a good growth of wispy Smoke Trees, a few sprawling Screwbean Mesquites and the occasional Indian Paintbrush plant. A long-tailed Roadrunner launched itself across the sand of the wash and stopped abruptly. An American **MORNING GLORY** cuckoo — yep, that's what a Roadrunner is — cocked his head at me as if to enquire, What's a strange animal like you doing on my turf? No answer from me. The Roadrunner stretched himself into a two-foot, horizontal streak of beak, feathers and tail and raced across the wash and out of sight. To a lizard hunter, men are no more than a stop-and-go distraction. I turned into a little arroyo. Within five minutes, the arroyo's mud banks — carved in the desert by winter rain flooding down from the mountains — had become three-foot walls. Growing up the mud wall and onto the sandy bank was a spreading Morning Glory that had used its vines and tentacles to carpet a section of the bank with green, heart-shaped leaves. The lavender trumpet flowers of the Morning Glory were robust and beautiful. Living up to their name. But as the sun reached its zenith, the Morning Glory blossoms would fade and wilt until another day.

I'm always surprised to find Morning Glories in the desert. Somehow they look out-of-place, orphans strayed from an urban garden wall. But wild Morning Glories grow just about everywhere in the United States. The moral, if there is one: When you go walking for flowers, leave your prejudices at home. The mighty Aztecs of Mexico had different reasons for admiring the

The Greek word for Morning Glory is Ipomoea, meaning wormlike. That doesn't refer to the beauty of the flower, which is well established. Worm-like refers to the plant's manner of locomotion. This Arizona Morning Glory, EVOLVULUS ARIZONICUS, uses its viney stems to crawl up, and around other plants and most anything else within its growth range.

Morning Glory. They had discovered that Morning Glory seeds, like Peyote Buttons, are hallucinogenic. Chewing the seeds was a social practice. After the effect had worn off, Aztec men gathered to exchange stories of the visions that had come to them from the dreams of Morning Glory seed.

Interesting, yes. But people do reach a state of exaltation — the vocabulary-starved 1960's called it a "high" — through the mere act of observing the unpredictable combination of form, shape, and color that turns an object such as a Morning Glory into a thing of beauty.

Another thing of beauty, but not to be touched, is the Prickly Pear Cactus. I read the book on Prickly Pear Cactus before I went up against one. So I carefully avoided the long, sharp needles as I reached in to take the blushing fruit growing on the edge of a slab-like leaf. What I harvested, instead of the fruit, was a handful of stinging nettles. My hand had become a magnet for glochids, the miniature spines **PRICKLY PEAR** that can hardly be seen without magnification. I was not alarmed, even though a stinging throb was vibrating through my fingers and thumb. Not alarmed because I always go prepared into the desert. My Swiss army knife has a pair of tweezers concealed in the handle. With the tweezers and the help of a field loupe — a handy instrument for examining bugs and flower parts and marveling **PRICKLY PEAR** at the whorls in your own fingerprints — I went to work on the glochids. When I clamped one with the tweezers, it didn't come out. It just broke off. What I should have said in the previous paragraph is I try to be prepared. Two or three days later, the glochids had apparently worked out through the skin. In the meantime, touching anything was painful.

Flowers of the Prickly Pear are of exceptional beauty, perhaps because they are in such sharp contrast to the bristling beast they spring from. One day in the desert, my pathfinder — a nest-building Cactus Wren — lead me to a

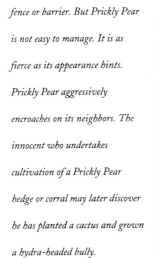

Prickly Pear is a plant of many virtues. It grows on most any kind of soil in most any arid or temperate climate. Its flowers are variously yellow, pink, purple, orange and red. Indians ate the inner part of Prickly Pear leaves as well as the tuna. Ranchers planted it as a fence or barrier. But Prickly Pear is not easy to manage. It is as fierce as its appearance hints. Prickly Pear aggressively encroaches on its neighbors. The innocent who undertakes cultivation of a Prickly Pear hedge or corral may later discover he has planted a cactus and grown a hydra-headed bully.

Prickly Pear plants have a life maximum of about twenty years. The fruit of the Prickly Pear — sometimes called Indian Fig, but known in the Spanish-speaking Southwest as tuna — is highly prized. And highly priced — last October my supermarket had tuna at $1.49 for one three-ounce fruit.

Prickly Pear in bloom. If a wren to you means the diminutive, bobbing House Wren, common east of the Rockies, a Cactus Wren may strike you as an imposter. I watched the Cactus Wren collecting dried grass and flying away with beaksful. I followed the bird, biggest of the wrens, to its building site. It had almost completed its nest among the thorns and glochids of a large, many-leaved Prickly Pear. The nest was a football-shaped house of straw. The wren had left a neat, wren-size porthole at one side. Yellow, cup-shaped flowers grew in profusion on the Prickly Pear. Silky flowers were elevated above the cactus leaves — as if for better display — on green ovals that would later ripen into tuna.

The beauty of flowers like the Prickly Pear and Hedgehog Cactus have inspired design motifs for artifacts crafted by many of the indigenous desert people. I traveled through the majestic Painted Desert in the 1930's on old U.S. Highway 66. Place names on that fabled road still glow with the luminescence of remembered youth — Gallup, Sanders, Petrified Forest, Navajo, Joseph City, Meteor Crater, Flagstaff. It was the decade of the Great American Depression. But even in the worst of economic times, optimistic boosters from Chicago to Santa Monica were beating the drums for "Highway 66, the Main Street of America." In those days of relative innocence, "Main Street" was a code name for "business," and business was as American as Mom and apple pie.

The long-needled Strawberry Hedgehog Cactus, ECHINOCEREUS ENGELMANNII, is truly a thorny bouquet. Its spectacular blossoms, **HEDGEHOG CACTUS** *ranging in color from vibrant magenta to pale pink, are nestled among a nest of sharp yellow spines.*

"The Main Street of America" skirted the southern section of the Painted Desert, and was the principal route for tourist access to the wonders of the "Indian" country — Navajo and Hopi reservations to the north and Apache reservations on the south. I remember stopping at a Navajo stand beside the highway. It was a brush lean-to. A hanging blanket was the only indication that the lean-to was a roadside business. Two women tended the primitive shop, and two children squatted unmoving in the rear of the lean-to. The younger of the two women sat before a ground cloth covered with a dozen pieces of turquoise and silver jewelry. She said her mother, a grandmotherly woman with leathery, wrinkled face, was the weaver of the blanket and of a smaller piece, a serape. The grandmother did not speak.

I counted the colors in the blanket and serape. Then I re-counted them. It did not seem possible that those hand-woven pieces could be so dazzlingly beautiful and yet contain only

Many Native Americans, like the Navajo and the Pueblo, use different plants, minerals, insects and animals to produce dyes for coloring wool, leather, baskets and pottery. Colors, as well as design motifs, have symbolic meaning: red represents life and the sun; yellow and orange depict the sunset; black represents joy or rain; and white symbolizes the dawn, or the beginning.

RED

Sumac, RHUS MICROPHYLLA, produces many colors from reddish brown to purple, gray, gold and dark brown depending on whether the fruit, leaves or twigs are used. Many Native American tribes used sumac for dyeing wool, basketry, tanning skins and porcupine quills.

YELLOW AND GOLD

Rabbit Brush, CHRYSOTHAMNUS spp. Its flowering tops combined with clay rich in alum produces a bright to deep yellow color.

GREEN

Morning Glory, IPOMOEA spp. Its fresh flowers boiled with alum as a mordant produces a green dye.

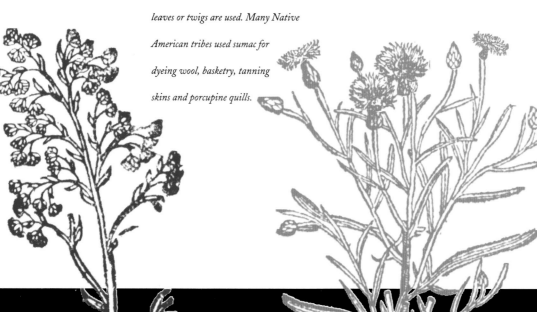

Many dyes are produced using naturally occurring mordants, a substance that helps enrich the color and set the dye. Some of the mordants used are native alum or alunite found in desert areas near sulfur springs, like Alum root (HEUCHERA spp.); iron salts which are found in many clays and muds in creeks and springs; gall nuts (oak galls which are a source of tannin); club moss and lichens; and even animal dung and urine.

BLUE

Indigo, INDIGOFERA LEPTOSEPALA, produces a rich dark blue dye when fermented for two weeks in urine.

BLACK

Indian Paintbrush, CASTILLEJA INTEGRA, the bark of its root used with minerals, produces a strong black color used for dyeing buckskin and some wools. Sumac, RHUS spp., its leaves and twigs processed with yellow ocher and Pinyon pine gum are used to dye wool and leather a rich deep black color.

BROWN

Sunflower, HELIANTHUS spp., produces a rich tan-brown color when the flower-heads were boiled in water with wool.

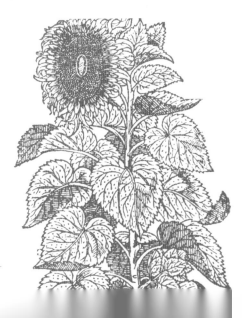

four colors, and only one of them a bright color: white, tan, brown and red. The secret, of course, was in the Navajo genius for design. The prices were $25 for the blanket and $15 for the serape. My ability to buy a blanket would have been about the same if the price had been $2,500. Today, those two masterpieces of Navajo artistry — or similar blankets — are probably stored in the vault of an Indian gallery in Santa Fe, Scottsdale, or Palm Springs. The prices per pound of those Navajo treasures — works of high art — might well approach the price per carat of cut diamonds.

Over the years, I have collected information about Indian blankets. No organized, scholarly research. More like remembered trivia. Only married women are permitted to become weavers. Their inspiration is Spider Woman, a figure of legend. Navajo rugs have no specific size — each rug is a reflection of the reach of the weaver. Designs are never drawn on paper; the weaver plots the design in her mind for many months before sitting down at the loom.

Nestled between rock and shale, the Butterweed, SENECIO sp.,

BUTTERWEED *presents itself in a flush of yellow flowers. The bright yellow flower heads bloom in loosely branched clusters on branched stalks well above the rich green foliage.*

The subject of dyes used to produce colors in traditional blankets and baskets is complicated. Black, white, and shades of brown were natural colors. Yarn of those colors was woven from the wool of sheep raised by the natives of the Painted Desert. Plants and flowers were used for dyes before chemical dyes became commonplace. For example, the Hopi used the seed husks of sunflower seeds and maize kernels to produce a range of red, purple and blue dyes. Dried black beans produced a black dye. But for bright red, the native weavers unwound the yarn in an English wool flannel called "bayeta." They bought "bayeta" by the piece from traders. An expert on Indian fabrics can tell "bayeta" yarn by appearance and feel. It has a tighter twist than locally-twisted yarn and it is uneven because it remembers the weave of its original use.

There is certainly no limit in nature's palette of colors and she displays them most prominently in spring. Splashes of vibrant Butterweed yellow, Claret Cup red and Morning Glory blue color the desert canvas. The first sighting of a many-flowered Serviceberry shrub is good news for me. Good news because it means the sap is running and nature is kicking in another turn at spring — most spectacular of the desert seasons. The oval shamrock-green leaves of the hardy shrub form the perfect backdrop for the five-petaled white flowers that are among the first of spring.

A profusion of delicate white flowers bloom on the thornless branches of the Serviceberry, AMELANCHIER sp. The fruit, a small purple, apple-shaped berry, ripens in late summer or autumn. Native Americans used the fruit in **SERVICEBERRY** *making* pemmican, *a frontier "trail mix." The women ground jerky into a powder, added Serviceberries and stuffed the mixture into rawhide bags. Then melted animal fat was added to penetrate and seal the mixture. The fat solidified and the* pemmican, *a concentrated food of high nutrition, was ready for the trail.*

Serviceberry is one of the many plants born with an uncertainty about its future. Shall I be a bush? Shall I be a tree? Usually it opts for bushdom, four to ten feet of green with a most generous shower of clustered flowers, each growing from a small cup. Then again, the plant decides to reach for the sun and becomes a tree. Even a thirty-foot tree. Whichever road it takes, bush or tree, Serviceberry produces a bountiful crop of fruit.

The berry plays a heroic role in the exploration and settlement of the American West. No word short of "heroic" is adequate to describe this berry. Can you imagine such a berry in a free-fall decline from favor? Serviceberry fruit is in such a decline. Dried Serviceberry fruit was the favored berry used in preparation of pemmican. Pemmican was to mountain men and Western explorers what MRE (Meal, Ready to Eat) is to the soldier of today — a portable, nutritious, easy-to-prepare, but not very tasty, ration. Maybe that explains the berry's fall from favor. None the less, Kit Carson, Jim Bridger, Hugh Glass, Meriwether Lewis, William Clark, the Roubidoux brothers, John Charles Fremont, and a host of other western traders, trappers, explorers and mountain men counted on pemmican to sustain them in hard marches through starvation country.

Whenever I see a Serviceberry bush in the Fall with a few dried berries still clinging to the stems, I think of pemmican. And I think, somebody should build a monument — on a hot butte of the high desert, or in a snowy pass of the Rockies — a monument to this nearly-forgotten berry. But when I see a Serviceberry in full, glorious bloom in the spring, I change my mind. I think, nope, no bronze and stone markers. The white-flowered Serviceberry bush is its own greatest monument.